BE

DYNAMIC

BE
DYNAMIC
EXPERIENCE THE POWER OF GOD'S PEOPLE

NT COMMENTARY
ACTS 1—12

Warren W. Wiersbe

David C Cook®
transforming lives together

BE DYNAMIC
Published by David C Cook
4050 Lee Vance View
Colorado Springs, CO 80918 U.S.A.

David C Cook U.K., Kingsway Communications
Eastbourne, East Sussex BN23 6NT, England

The graphic circle C logo is a registered trademark of David C Cook.

Unless otherwise noted, all Scripture quotations are taken from the King James Version of the Bible. (Public Domain.) Scripture quotations marked NASB are taken from the *New American Standard Bible,* © Copyright 1960, 1995 by The Lockman Foundation. Used by permission; NKJV are taken from the New King James Version. Copyright © 1982 by Thomas Nelson, Inc. Used by permission. All rights reserved; and NIV are taken from the *Holy Bible, New International Version®. NIV®.* Copyright © 1973, 1978, 1984 International Bible Society. Used by permission of Zondervan. All rights reserved; and WUEST are taken from *The New Testament: An Expanded Translation* by Kenneth S. Wuest, © 1961 by Wm. B. Eerdmans Publishing Company. Italics in Scripture have been added by the author for emphasis.

LCCN 2009923012
ISBN 978-1-4347-6746-2
eISBN 978-1-4347-0020-9

First edition of *Be Dynamic* by Warren W. Wiersbe published by Victor Books®
in 1987 © Warren W. Wiersbe, ISBN 0-89693-358-X

The Team: Karen Lee-Thorp, Amy Kiechlin, Jack Campbell, and Susan Vannaman
Series Cover Design: John Hamilton Design
Cover Photo: Veer Images

Printed in the United States of America
Second Edition 2009

9 10 11 12 13 14 15 16 17 18

041516

This book is for some missionary friends who have challenged and enriched our lives and whose ministries have extended the church:

Paul and Kathie Buyse
Don and Alene Dix
Don and Vera Hillis
Abe and Marj Van Der Puy

CONTENTS

THE BIG IDEA

An Introduction to *Be Dynamic*
by Ken Baugh

Twenty-three years ago, my wife and I were sitting in our car parked in front of a beach in Malibu, California, watching the waves and eating our quarter pounders with cheese (that was when I could eat a quarter pounder without looking like one). We were on our honeymoon, and as we were sitting in the car, basking in our love for each other, I noticed a homeless man moseying around on the beach. He finally sat down by a trash can directly in front of our car.

My sweet wife suggested that I go over and share Christ with this man, but to be honest, that wasn't my first thought. I was more interested in finishing my burger and fries than I was in the eternal destiny of this man. But then, being the incredibly intuitive person that I am (yes, I'm being sarcastic), I realized that this was a test. My wife wanted to see what kind of spiritual stuff her new husband was made of. So, being the spiritual giant that I am (again, I jest), I told her that I would love to go over and share Christ with this man, but I didn't have an evangelistic tract or Bible to use. I thought this would get me off the hook. But to my chagrin, Susan just happened to have a *Four Spiritual Laws* booklet in her purse. Now

I was on the spot, so I relented, set down my burger and fries, took one last slurp from my Coke, got out of the car, and walked over to where the homeless man was sitting.

His name was Paul, and I asked him if I could sit down and talk with him. He said, "Sure." As we talked, I found out that at one time he had been a prominent businessman but had lost everything, including his wife and family, so he just dropped out of normal life. Paul's story was truly tragic. As we talked, I slowly steered the conversation toward spiritual matters and gently shared the gospel with him. He was fairly polite but not very interested in continuing our dialogue, so after about ten to fifteen minutes, I thanked him for taking the time to talk with me, gave him the booklet, and wished him well.

As I walked back to the car, I saw my new bride beaming with pride, thinking that her new husband was a bold and dynamic man of God, willing to share the gospel with a total stranger. But I knew the truth about myself: that I would never have taken the initiative to talk to Paul without Susan's prompting. You see, twenty-three years ago it was difficult for me to share my faith with strangers. And to be honest, even today after I've been in ministry for over twenty years, it's still difficult.

Yet the mandate of the Great Commission to go and make disciples of all people groups is a command for every true follower of Christ, not just for those who have the gift of evangelism. God wants every disciple to be a dynamic witness for Him. This is the Big Idea that runs throughout the first twelve chapters of the book of Acts. Peter was just a fisherman, untrained in the fine details of theology, yet the Holy Spirit used him in dynamic ways to bring many people to a saving faith in Jesus as the Messiah.

So here's my question: How can we be like Peter and share our faith with others in effective ways even when we're scared and may not really want to? The answer lies in knowing how to use four tools of evangelism:

service evangelism, lifestyle evangelism, friendship evangelism, and confrontational evangelism. Let's open up our evangelism toolbox and learn how to use each one effectively.

Tool #1: Service Evangelism. Think of service evangelism as a way of sharing the love of Christ with others in practical ways that meet specific felt needs. It's giving that cup of cold water to someone who is thirsty (see Matt. 10:42). Now, the difference between humanitarian aid and service evangelism projects is that humanitarian aid doesn't typically share openly about the person and work of Jesus Christ, but in service evangelism you do. And as you serve people, with no strings attached, you will quickly discover that they ask you why you are helping them, and this gives you the opportunity to share the gospel: "I'm just sharing God's love in a practical way. Can we talk about Jesus?" Recently, I was part of a team from our church that brought aid to those affected by Hurricane Ike in Galveston, Texas. We had our food-pantry truck with us, and we went to Walmart and loaded it up with water, drinks, socks, T-shirts, blankets, and food items and drove to a campsite where there were dozens of people living in tents who had been displaced by the hurricane. As we were handing out these goods to the people, they were both grateful and inquisitive as to why we were helping them, and it gave us a great opportunity to share with them the love of Christ. So service evangelism is a simple way to meet human needs while talking about Jesus.

Tool #2: Lifestyle Evangelism. This means of evangelism is based upon Jesus' words to be light in the world (see Matt. 5:14). To be the light that Jesus is referring to simply means that as a Christian, I am to reflect who Jesus is to others. For example, the moon has no ability to generate light on its own; it simply reflects the light of the sun. In the same way, as believers, we are to reflect the light of Christ's love, mercy, and kindness to others everywhere we go. No doubt you've heard some variation of this illustration: "If you were put on trial because of your claim to be a

Christian, would there be enough evidence to convict you?" That's what we're talking about in lifestyle evangelism, living out the faith in such a way that others see the difference and ask you about it.

Tool #3: Friendship Evangelism. A few years ago, I was working with a trainer down at my local gym. He knew I was a pastor, but I never brought it up. Instead I was willing to wait and see what might happen. One day after a few weeks, I was in the middle of a set, lifting a couple of very heavy dumbbells, when he just blurted out, "So what's the deal about Christians believing that Jesus is God?" I was so surprised, I almost dropped the weights on my head. For some reason, my trainer felt safe enough because of our growing friendship to ask me a spiritual question that had been on his mind for a long time. I think friendship evangelism operates in a similar way to another statement Jesus made about Christians: We are to be salt in the world (see Matt. 5:13). Salt was used to preserve meat without the aid of refrigeration, and salt is also a flavor enhancer. I believe as we build relationships with unbelievers, and they get to know us and we them, our friendship can act like a flavor enhancer bringing out the God flavors of His Word. I like how *The Message* version of the Bible puts it: "Let me tell you why you are here. You're here to be salt-seasoning that brings out the God-flavors of this earth" (Matt. 5:13). When a believer becomes friends with an unbeliever, their friendship becomes a God-ordained flavor enhancer that draws them to Christ.

Tool #4: Confrontational Evangelism. I consider most street preachers to be fairly confrontational in their approach to evangelism. I used to be really turned off and even embarrassed by their approach. However, I have come to believe that street preaching can be very effective. My good friend Lon Solomon, pastor of McLean Bible Church, became a Christian through the ministry of a street preacher while he was attending the University of North Carolina. Today, Lon has a thriving ministry in the Washington D.C. area, including a weekly radio broadcast that takes the gospel to tens of thousands of people each week, and all because a street preacher was bold enough to proclaim the gospel in a direct and compelling way. The confrontational approach isn't for everybody, and it certainly isn't the most effective tool in every situation, but it sure works in the right context.

So now you have a full toolbox of evangelistic tools that you can choose from, depending on the situation you find yourself in. Just remember, God doesn't call you as a Christian to save people, just to sow the seed of the gospel. And as you do, the Holy Spirit will do the rest of the work, drawing people into relationship with Jesus Christ in dynamic ways.

***

Dr. Wiersbe's commentaries have been a source of guidance and strength to me over the many years that I have been a pastor. His unique style is not overly academic, but theologically sound. He explains the deep truths of Scripture in a way that everyone can understand and apply. Whether you're a Bible scholar or a brand-new believer in Christ, you will benefit, as I have, from Warren's insights. With your Bible in one hand and Dr. Wiersbe's commentary in the other, you will be able to accurately unpack the deep truths of God's Word and learn how to apply them to your life.

Drink deeply, my friend, of the truths of God's Word, for in them you will find Jesus Christ, and there is freedom, peace, assurance, and joy.

—Ken Baugh
Pastor of Coast Hills Community Church
Alison Viejo, California

A WORD FROM THE AUTHOR

We call Dr. Luke's second volume "The Acts of the Apostles," when really it is the "Acts of God's People Empowered by the Holy Spirit." It is a story of power.

That's why I have called this book *Be Dynamic*. I think Dr. Luke would approve; for, after all, God's people today share the same spiritual dynamic that energized the early saints. If we are yielded to the Spirit, we can be adding new chapters to the exciting story of the church.

There are some nonrepeatable events in Acts, as well as some transitional happenings; but the basic spiritual principles are the same today as when Peter and Paul ministered.

We need to look beyond the accidentals to the essentials and discover afresh the spiritual dynamics of the Word of God and prayer, love and fellowship, persecution, and personal witness for Christ.

Vance Havner used to say that our church services start at eleven o'clock sharp and end at twelve o'clock dull. But it doesn't have to be that way. If we will lay hold of the "power principles" recorded in Acts, we can be dynamic and see our local churches do exploits for the Lord.

I trust that your study of the book of Acts will do that for you and your church.

—Warren W. Wiersbe

A Suggested Outline of the Book of Acts

Theme: The expansion of the church in the world
Key verse: Acts 1:8

I. The Ministry of Peter (Acts 1—12)

   1. Jerusalem the center

   2. Ministry primarily to Israel

      A. Peter and the Jews (Acts 1—7)

      B. Peter and the Samaritans (Acts 8)

      C. The conversion of Paul (Acts 9)

      D. Peter and the Gentiles (Acts 10—11)

      E. Peter's arrest and deliverance (Acts 12)

II. The Ministry of Paul (Acts 13—28)

   1. Syrian Antioch the center

   2. Ministry primarily to the Gentiles

      A. Paul's first missionary journey (Acts 13—14)

      B. The Jerusalem Conference (Acts 15)

      C. Paul's second missionary journey (Acts 16:1—18:22)

      D. Paul's third missionary journey (Acts 18:23—21:17)

      E. Paul's arrest and voyage to Rome (Acts 21:18—28:31)

Chapter One

THE FAITH OF THE FIRST CHRISTIANS

(Acts 1)

A famous Hollywood producer once said that for a movie to be successful, it must start with an earthquake and work up to a climax. Luke certainly didn't follow that formula when he wrote the book of Acts. Except for the ascension of Jesus Christ, events recorded in Acts 1 are anything but dramatic. After all, what is exciting about a business meeting?

Then why record these events? Why didn't Luke just start with the story of Pentecost? For several reasons.

To begin with, Luke was writing volume two of a work that started with what we call the gospel of Luke (see Luke 1:1–4), and he had to begin with the proper salutation and introduction. We don't know who Theophilus was or even if he was a believer, but Luke's salutation suggests that he may have been an important Roman official (see Acts 23:26; 24:3; 26:25). Likely Theophilus was a Christian or at least a seeker who was carefully studying the Christian faith. His name means "friend of God," and we hope he lived up to his name.

But even more important, Luke had to build a bridge between his gospel and the book of Acts (Luke 24:50–53). At the close of his gospel, he had left the believers in the temple, praising God. Now he had to pick up the story and explain what happened next. Imagine how confused you would be if, in reading your New Testament, you turned the last page of the gospel of John and discovered—Romans! "How did the church get to Rome?" you would ask yourself; the answer is found in the book of Acts.

The book of Acts is also the account of the work of the Holy Spirit *in* and *through* the church. The gospel of Luke records what Jesus "began both to do and teach" in His human body, and the book of Acts tells us what Jesus *continued* to do and teach through His spiritual body, the church. Even today, congregations can learn much about church life and ministry from this book, and this even includes the business meetings!

In this chapter, we see the believers taking care of "unfinished business" and getting ready for Pentecost. What they said and did reveals to us the faith of the church. In what did they really believe?

THEY BELIEVED IN THE RISEN CHRIST (1:1–11)

After His resurrection, Jesus remained on earth for forty days and ministered to His disciples. He had already opened their minds to understand the Old Testament message about Himself (Luke 24:44–48), but there were other lessons they needed to learn before they could launch out in their new ministry. Jesus appeared and disappeared during those forty days, and the believers never knew when He might show up. It was excellent preparation for the church because the days were soon coming when He would no longer be on earth to instruct them personally. We believers today never know when our Lord may return, so our situation is somewhat similar to theirs.

The Lord taught them several important lessons during that time of special ministry.

The reality of His resurrection (v. 3a). Some of the believers may have had their doubts forty days before (Mark 16:9–14), but there could be no question now that Jesus had indeed been raised from the dead. To strengthen their faith, He gave them "many infallible proofs," which Luke did not explain. We know that when Jesus met His disciples, He invited them to touch His body, and He even ate before them (Luke 24:38–43). Whatever proofs He gave, they were convincing.

Faith in His resurrection was important to the church because their own spiritual power depended on it. Also, the message of the gospel involves the truth of the resurrection (Rom. 10:9–10; 1 Cor. 15:1–8), and if Jesus were dead, the church would be speechless. Finally, the official Jewish position was that the disciples had stolen Jesus' body from the tomb (Matt. 28:11–15), and the believers had to be able to refute this as they witnessed to the nation.

These believers were chosen to be special witnesses of Christ's resurrection, and that was the emphasis in their ministry (Acts 1:22; 2:32; 3:15; 5:30–32). Most of the people in Jerusalem knew that Jesus of Nazareth had been crucified, but they did not know that He had been raised from the dead. By their words, their walk, and their mighty works, the believers told the world that Jesus was alive. This was "the sign of Jonah" that Jesus had promised to the nation (Matt. 12:38–41)—His death, burial, and resurrection.

The coming of His kingdom (v. 3b). This refers to the reign of God over the hearts and lives of those who have trusted Him (see Matt. 6:33; Rom. 14:17; 1 John 3:1–9). When you read the four Gospels, you discover that the apostles had a strong political view of the kingdom and were especially concerned about their own positions and privileges. Being loyal Jews, they longed for the defeat of their enemies and the final establishment of the glorious kingdom under the rule of King Messiah. They did not realize that there must first be a spiritual change in the hearts of the people (see Luke 1:67–79).

Jesus did not rebuke them when they "kept asking" about the future

Jewish kingdom (Acts 1:7). After all, He had opened their minds to understand the Scriptures (Luke 24:44), so they knew what they were asking. But God has not revealed His timetable to us, and it is futile for us to speculate. The important thing is not to be curious about the future but to be busy in the present, sharing the message of God's *spiritual* kingdom. This is another emphasis in the book of Acts (see Acts 8:12; 14:22; 20:25; 28:23, 31).

The power of His Holy Spirit (vv. 4–8). John the Baptist had announced a future baptism of the Holy Spirit (Matt. 3:11; Mark 1:8; Luke 3:16; John 1:33; and see Acts 11:16), and now that prophecy would be fulfilled. Jesus had also promised the coming of the Spirit (John 14:16–18, 26; 15:26–27; 16:7–15). It would be an endowment of power for the disciples so that they would be able to serve the Lord and accomplish His will (Luke 24:49). John had spoken about "the Holy Spirit and fire," but Jesus said nothing about fire. Why? Because the "baptism of fire" has to do with future judgment, when the nation of Israel will go through tribulation (Matt. 3:11–12). The appearing of "tongues of fire" at Pentecost (Acts 2:3) could not be termed a "baptism."

Acts 1:8 is a key verse. To begin with, it explains that the power of the church comes from the Holy Spirit and not from man (see Zech. 4:6). God's people experienced repeated fillings of the Spirit as they faced new opportunities and obstacles (Acts 2:4; 4:8, 31; 9:17; 13:9). Ordinary people were able to do extraordinary things because the Spirit of God was at work in their lives. The ministry of the Holy Spirit is not a luxury; it is an absolute necessity.

Witness is a key word in the book of Acts and is used twenty-nine times as either a verb or a noun. A witness is somebody who tells what he has seen and heard (Acts 4:19–20). When you are on the witness stand in court, the judge is not interested in your ideas or opinions; he only wants to hear what you know. Our English word *martyr* comes from the Greek word translated "witness," and many of God's people have sealed their witness by laying down their lives.

We hear a great deal these days about "soul winning," and the emphasis is a good one. However, while *some* of God's people have a calling to evangelism (Eph. 4:11), *all* of God's people are expected to be witnesses and tell the lost about the Savior. Not every Christian can bring a sinner to the place of faith and decision (though most of us could do better), but every Christian can bear faithful witness to the Savior. "A true witness delivereth souls" (Prov. 14:25).

Acts 1:8 also gives us a general outline of the book of Acts as it describes the geographical spread of the gospel: from Jerusalem (Acts 1—7) to Judea and Samaria (Acts 8—9), and then to the Gentiles and to the ends of the earth (Acts 10—28). No matter where we live, as Christians we should begin our witness at home and then extend it "into all the world." As Dr. Oswald J. Smith used to say, "The light that shines the farthest will shine the brightest at home."

The assurance of His coming again (vv. 9–11). Our Lord's ascension into heaven was an important part of His ministry, for if He had not returned to the Father, He could not have sent the promised gift of the Holy Spirit (John 16:5–15). Also, in heaven today, the Savior is our interceding High Priest, giving us the grace that we need for life and service (Heb. 4:14–16). He is also our Advocate before the Father, forgiving us when we confess our sins (1 John 1:9—2:2). The exalted and glorified Head of the church is now working with His people on earth and helping them accomplish His purposes (Mark 16:19–20).

As the believers watched Jesus being taken up to glory, two angels appeared and gently rebuked them. Angels play an important role in the ministry described in Acts, just as they do today, even though we cannot see them (see Acts 5:19–20; 8:26; 10:3–7; 12:7–10, 23; 27:23). The angels are the servants of the saints (Heb. 1:14).

The two messengers gave the believers assurance that Jesus Christ would come again, just as He had been taken from them. This seems to refer to His public "coming in the clouds" (Matt. 24:30; 26:64; Rev. 1:7) rather than to His coming for His church "in a moment, in the twinkling of an eye" (1 Cor. 15:51–52; 1 Thess. 4:13–18). Regardless of what views different people may take of God's prophetic program, Christians agree that Jesus is coming again and that He can come at any time. This in itself is a great motivation for faithful Christian service (Luke 12:34–48).

They Believed in Each Other (1:12–14)

They obeyed their Lord's commandment and returned to Jerusalem "with great joy" (Luke 24:52). It is likely that the group met in the upper room where the last Passover had been celebrated, but they were also found at worship in the temple (v. 53).

What a variety of people made up that first assembly of believers! There were men and women, apostles and "ordinary" people, and even members of the Lord's earthly family (see Matt. 13:55; Mark 6:3). His "brethren" had not believed in Him during His ministry (John 7:5), but they did come to trust Him after the resurrection (Acts 1:14). Mary was there as a member of the assembly, participating in worship and prayer along with the others. The center of their fellowship was the risen Christ, and all of them adored and magnified Him.

How easy it would have been for someone to bring division into this beautiful assembly of humble people! The members of the Lord's family might have claimed special recognition, or Peter could have been criticized for his cowardly denial of the Savior. Or perhaps Peter might have blamed John because it was John who brought him into the high priest's house (John 18:15–16). John might well have reminded the others that *he* had faithfully stood at the cross, and had even been chosen by the Savior to care for His mother. But there was none of this. In fact, nobody was even arguing over who among them was the greatest!

The key phrase is "with one accord," a phrase that is found six times in Acts (1:14; 2:1, 46; 4:24; 5:12; 15:25; and note also 2:44). There was among these believers a wonderful unity that bound them together in Christ (Ps. 133; Gal. 3:28), the kind of unity that Christians need today. "I do not want the walls of separation between different orders of Christians to be destroyed," said the godly British preacher Rowland Hill, "but only lowered, that we may shake hands a little easier over them!"

It is not enough for Christians to have faith in the Lord; they must also have faith in one another. To these 120 people (Acts 1:15) the Lord had given the solemn responsibility of bearing witness to a lost world, and none of them could do the job alone. They would experience severe persecution in the days ahead, and one of them, James, would lay down his life for Christ. It was not a time for asking, "Who is the greatest?" or, "Who committed the greatest sin?" It was a time for praying together and standing together in the Lord. As they waited and worshipped together, they were being better prepared for the work that lay before them.

THEY BELIEVED IN PRAYER (1:15, 24–25)

Prayer plays a significant role in the story of the church as recorded in the book of Acts. The believers prayed for guidance in making decisions (Acts 1:15–26) and for courage to witness for Christ (4:23–31). In fact, prayer was a normal part of their daily ministry (2:42–47; 3:1; 6:4). Stephen prayed as he was being stoned (7:55–60). Peter and John prayed for the Samaritans (8:14–17), and Saul of Tarsus prayed after his conversion (9:11). Peter prayed before he raised Dorcas from the dead (vv. 36–43). Cornelius prayed that God would show him how to be saved (1–4), and Peter was on the housetop praying when God told him how to be the answer to Cornelius's prayers (v. 9).

The believers in John Mark's house prayed for Peter when he was in prison, and the Lord delivered him both from prison and from death (Acts 12:1–11). The church at Antioch fasted and prayed before sending out Barnabas and Paul (13:1–3; and note 14:23). It was at a prayer meeting in Philippi that God opened Lydia's heart (16:13), and another prayer meeting in Philippi opened the prison doors (v. 16:25ff.). Paul prayed for his friends before leaving them (20:36; 21:5). In the midst of a storm, he prayed for God's blessing (27:35), and after a storm, he prayed that God would heal a sick man (28:8). In almost every chapter in Acts you find a reference to prayer, and the book makes it very clear that something happens when God's people pray.

This is certainly a good lesson for the church today. Prayer is both the thermometer and the thermostat of the local church, for the "spiritual temperature" either goes up or down, depending on how God's people pray. John Bunyan, author of *Pilgrim's Progress,* said, "Prayer is a shield to the soul, a sacrifice to God, and a scourge to Satan." In the book of Acts, you see prayer accomplishing all of these things.

THEY BELIEVED IN GOD'S LEADING (1:16–23)

The Lord Jesus was no longer with them to give them personal directions, but they were not without the leading of the Lord, for they had the Word of God and prayer. In fact, the Word of God and prayer formed the foundation for the ministry of the church as recorded in the book of Acts (Acts 6:4).

Peter has been criticized for taking charge, but I believe he was doing the will of God. Jesus had made it clear that Peter was to be their leader (Matt. 16:19; Luke 22:31–32; John 21:15–17). Peter was "first among equals," but he was their recognized leader. His name is mentioned first in each listing of the apostles, including Acts 1:13.

But should Peter and the others have waited until the Spirit had been given? We must not forget that the Lord had previously "breathed" on them and imparted the Spirit to them (John 20:22). When the Spirit came at Pentecost, it was for the purpose of filling them with power and baptizing them into one body in Christ.

We must also remember that the Lord had opened up their minds to understand the Scriptures (Luke 24:45). When Peter referred to Psalms 69:25 and 109:8, he was not doing this on his own, but was being led by the Spirit of God. These people definitely believed in the divine inspiration of the Old Testament Scriptures (Acts 1:16; and see 3:18; 4:25), and they also believed that these Scriptures had a practical application to their situation.

A radio listener once wrote to ask me, "Why do you teach from the Old Testament? After all, it's ancient history and it's all been fulfilled by Jesus!" I explained that the only "Bible" the early church had was the Old Testament, and yet they were able to use it to discover the will of God. We need both the Old and the New; in fact, the New Testament writers often quote from the Old Testament to prove their point. St. Augustine said, "The New is in the Old concealed; the Old is by the New revealed."

Certainly we must interpret the Old by the New, but we must not think that God no longer speaks to His people through the Old Testament Scriptures. "*All* Scripture is given by inspiration of God, and is profitable" (2 Tim. 3:16). "Man shall not live by bread alone, but by *every* word that proceedeth out of the mouth of God" (Matt. 4:4). We must use the whole Bible and balance Scripture with Scripture as we seek to discover the mind of God.

"But it was wrong for them to select a new apostle," some claim, "because Paul was the one who was chosen by God to fill up the ranks. They chose Matthias and he was never heard of again!"

Except for Peter and John, *none of the original Twelve* are mentioned by name in the book of Acts after 1:13! Paul could not have "filled up the ranks" because he could never have met the divine qualifications laid down in Acts 1:21–22. Paul was not baptized by John the Baptist; he did not travel with the apostles when Jesus was with them on earth; and though he saw the glorified Christ, Paul was not a witness of the resurrection as were the original apostles.

Paul made it clear that he was *not* to be classified with the Twelve (1 Cor. 15:8; Gal. 1:15–24), and the Twelve knew it. If the Twelve thought that Paul was supposed to be one of them, they certainly did not show it! In fact, they refused to admit Paul into the Jerusalem fellowship until Barnabas came to his rescue (Acts 9:26–27)! The twelve apostles ministered primarily to the twelve tribes of Israel, while Paul was sent to the Gentiles (Gal. 2:1–10).

No, Paul was not meant to be the twelfth apostle. Peter and the other believers were in the will of God when they selected Matthias, and God gave His endorsement to Matthias by empowering him with the same Spirit that was given to the other men whom Jesus had personally selected (Acts 2:1–4, 14).

It was necessary that twelve men witness at Pentecost to the twelve tribes of Israel, and also that twelve men be prepared to sit on twelve thrones to judge the twelve tribes (Luke 22:28–30). From Acts 2—7, the witness was primarily to Israel, "to the Jew first" (see Rom. 1:16; Acts 3:26; 13:46). Once the message had gone to the Gentiles (Acts 10—11), this Jewish emphasis began to decline. When the apostle James was martyred, he was not replaced (Acts 12). Why? Because the official witness to Israel was now completed, and the message was going out to Jews and Gentiles alike. There was no more need for twelve apostles to give witness to the twelve tribes of Israel.

Peter's account of the purchase of the land and the death of Judas appears to contradict the record in Matthew 27:3–10, but actually it complements it. Judas did not buy the field personally, but since it was his money that paid for it, in that sense, he was the buyer. And, since the thirty pieces of silver were considered "blood money," the field was called "the field of blood" (Matt. 27:8). It was not Judas's blood that gave the field its name, for the Jews would not use as a sacred cemetery a place that had been defiled by a suicide. Judas hanged himself, and apparently the rope broke and his body (possibly already distended) burst open when it hit the ground.

The believers prayed for God's guidance before they "voted" because they wanted to select the man that God had already chosen (Prov. 16:33). Their exalted Lord was working in them and through them from heaven. This is the last instance in the Bible of the casting of lots, and there is no reason why believers today should use this approach in determining God's will. While it is not always easy to discover what God wants us to do, if we are willing to obey Him, He will reveal His will to us (John 7:17). What is important is that we follow the example of the early church by emphasizing the Word of God and prayer.

Not all our Lord's followers were in the upper room, for there were only 120 present and 1 Corinthians 15:6 states that at least 500 persons saw the risen Christ at one time. Bible scholars do not agree on the size of the population of Palestine at that time, and their estimates run from 600,000 to 4 million. But regardless of what figure you select, the 120 believers were still a minority, yet they turned their world upside down for Christ!

What was their secret? The power of the Holy Spirit!

Dr. Luke explains this in Acts 2.

QUESTIONS FOR PERSONAL REFLECTION
OR GROUP DISCUSSION

1. If you had to explain the word *power* with an object, what object would you use? Why?

2. The book of Acts is the story of God's power through His believers. Read Luke 24:44–53 and Acts 1:1–11. How is Acts a continuation of Luke's gospel?

3. What did Jesus teach about the relationship between His resurrection and the indwelling of the Holy Spirit?

4. What is the relationship between Christ's resurrection and the responsibility of being witnesses?

5. Read Acts 1:12–26. How does faith in the resurrected Christ affect our unity?

6. How does faith in Christ affect our prayer lives?

7. What is the correlation between faith and our knowledge of God's will?

8. What is the difference between an intellectual understanding of Christ's resurrection and faith in the resurrected Christ?

9. How would you evaluate your faith in Christ?

10. What can you do this week to strengthen your faith in the resurrected Christ?

Chapter Two

POWER FROM HEAVEN!

(Acts 2)

W e are not going to move this world by criticism of it nor conformity to it, but by the combustion within it of lives ignited by the Spirit of God."

Vance Havner made that statement and he was right. The early church had none of the things that we think are so essential for success today—buildings, money, political influence, social status—and yet the church won multitudes to Christ and saw many churches established throughout the Roman world. Why? Because the church had the power of the Holy Spirit energizing its ministry. They were a people who "were ignited by the Spirit of God."

That same Holy Spirit power is available to us today to make us more effective witnesses for Christ. The better we understand His working at Pentecost, the better we will be able to relate to Him and experience His power. The ministry of the Spirit is to glorify Christ in the life and witness of the believer (John 16:14), and that is what is important. Acts 2 helps us understand the Holy Spirit by recording four experiences in the life of the church.

THE CHURCH WAITING FOR THE SPIRIT (2:1)

Pentecost means "fiftieth" because this feast was held fifty days after the Feast of Firstfruits (Lev. 23:15–22). The calendar of Jewish feasts in Leviticus 23 is an outline of the work of Jesus Christ. Passover pictures His death as the Lamb of God (John 1:29; 1 Cor. 5:7), and the Feast of Firstfruits pictures His resurrection from the dead (1 Cor. 15:20–23). Fifty days after Firstfruits is the Feast of Pentecost, which pictures the formation of the church. At Pentecost, the Jews celebrated the giving of the law, but Christians celebrate it because of the giving of the Holy Spirit to the church.

The Feast of Firstfruits took place on the day after the Sabbath following Passover, which means it was always on the first day of the week. (The Sabbath is the seventh day.) Jesus arose from the dead on the first day of the week and "became the firstfruits of them that slept" (1 Cor. 15:20). Now, if Pentecost was fifty days later—seven weeks plus one day—then Pentecost also took place on the first day of the week. Christians assemble and worship on Sunday, the first day of the week, because on that day our Lord arose from the dead, but it was also the day on which the Holy Spirit was given to the church.

On the Feast of Firstfruits, the priest waved a sheaf of grain before the Lord, but on Pentecost, he presented two loaves of bread. Why? Because at Pentecost, the Holy Spirit baptized the believers and united them into one body. The Jewish believers received this baptism at Pentecost, and the Gentile believers received this baptism in the home of Cornelius (Acts 10). This explains the presence of two loaves of bread (see 1 Cor. 10:17). The fact that there was leaven (yeast) in the loaves indicates the presence of sin in the church on earth. The church will not be perfect until it gets to heaven.

We must not conclude that this ten-day prayer meeting brought about the miracles of Pentecost, or that we today may pray as they did and experience "another Pentecost." Like our Lord's death at Calvary, Pentecost was a once-for-all event that will not be repeated. The church may experience new fillings of the Spirit, and certainly patient prayer is an essential element to spiritual power, but we would not ask for another Pentecost any more than we would ask for another Calvary.

THE CHURCH WORSHIPPING THE LORD (2:2–13)

As we study the events of Pentecost, it is important that we separate the accidentals from the essentials. The Spirit *came* and the people heard the sound of rushing wind and saw tongues of fire. The Spirit *baptized* and *filled* the believers, and then *spoke* as they praised God in various languages. The Spirit *empowered* Peter to preach, and then He *convicted* the listeners so that three thousand of them trusted Christ and were saved. Let's consider these ministries one by one.

The Spirit came (vv. 2–3). The Holy Spirit had been active prior to Pentecost and had worked in creation (Gen. 1:1–2), in Old Testament history (Judg. 6:34; 1 Sam. 16:13), and in the life and ministry of Jesus (Luke 1:30–37; 4:1, 14; Acts 10:38). However, now there would be two changes: The Spirit would dwell in people and not just come on them, and His presence would be permanent, not temporary (John 14:16–17). The Spirit could not have come sooner, for it was essential that Jesus die, be raised from the dead, and return to heaven before the Spirit could be given (John 7:37–39; 16:7ff.). Remember the Jewish calendar in Leviticus 23: Passover, Firstfruits, and then Pentecost.

There were three startling signs that accompanied the coming of the Spirit: the sound of a rushing wind, tongues of fire, and the believers praising God in various languages. The word *Spirit* is the same as "wind" in both the Hebrew and the Greek (John 3:8). The people did not *feel* the wind; they heard *the sound* of a mighty wind. It is likely the believers were in the temple when this occurred (Luke 24:53). The word *house* in Acts 2:2

can refer to the temple (see Acts 7:47). The tongues of fire symbolized the powerful witness of the church to the people. Campbell Morgan reminds us that our tongues can be set on fire either by heaven or by hell (James 3:5–6)! Combine wind and fire and you have—a blaze!

The Spirit baptized (1:5). The Greek word *baptizo* has two meanings, one literal and the other figurative. The word literally means "to submerge," but the figurative meaning is "to be identified with." The baptism of the Spirit is that act of God by which He identified believers with the exalted Head of the church, Jesus Christ, and formed the spiritual body of Christ on earth (1 Cor. 12:12–14). Historically, this took place at Pentecost; today, it takes place whenever a sinner trusts Jesus Christ and is born again.

When you read about "baptism" in the New Testament, you must exercise discernment to determine whether the word is to be interpreted literally or symbolically. For example, in Romans 6:3–4 and Galatians 3:27–28, the reference is symbolic since water baptism cannot put a sinner into Jesus Christ. Only the Holy Spirit can do that (Rom. 8:9; 1 Cor. 12:13; see Acts 10:44–48). Water baptism is a public witness of the person's identification with Jesus Christ, while Spirit baptism is the personal and private experience that identifies the person with Christ.

It is important to note that historically, the baptism of the Spirit took place in two stages: The Jewish believers were baptized at Pentecost, and the Gentiles were baptized and added to the body in the home of Cornelius (Acts 10:44–48; 11:15–17; and see Eph. 2:11–22).

The Spirit filled (v. 4). The filling of the Spirit has to do with power for witness and service (Acts 1:8). We are not exhorted to be baptized by the Spirit, for this is something God does once and for all when we trust His Son. But we are commanded to be filled with the Spirit (Eph. 5:18), for we need His power constantly if we are to serve God effectively. At Pentecost, the Christians were filled with the Spirit and experienced the baptism of the Spirit, but after that, they experienced many fillings (Acts 4:8, 31; 9:17; 13:9) but no more baptisms.

Occasionally someone says, "What difference does it make what words we use? The important thing is that we have the experience!" I doubt that they would apply that same approach to any other area of life such as medicine, cooking, or mechanics. What difference does it make if the pharmacist uses arsenic or aspirin in the prescription, just so long as you get well? Or if the mechanic installs an alternator or a carburetor, just so long as the car works?

The Holy Spirit has revealed God's truth to us in *words* (1 Cor. 2:12–13), and these words have definite meanings that must not be changed. Regeneration must not be confused with justification, nor propitiation with adoption. Each of these words is important in God's plan of salvation and must be defined accurately and used carefully.

The baptism of the Spirit means that I belong to His body; the fullness of the Spirit means that my body belongs to Him. The baptism is final; the fullness is repeated as we trust God for new power to witness. The baptism involves all other believers, for it makes us one in the body of Christ (Eph. 4:1–6); while the fullness is personal and individual. These are two distinct experiences and they must not be confused.

The Spirit spoke (vv. 5–13). Note that the believers were praising God, not preaching the gospel, and that they used known languages, not an "unknown tongue" (Acts 2:6, 8). Luke named fifteen different geographical locations and clearly stated that the citizens of those places heard Peter and the others declare God's wonderful works *in languages they could understand.* The Greek word translated "language" in Acts 2:6 and "tongue" in Acts 2:8 is *dialektos* and refers to a language or dialect of some country or district (Acts 21:40; 22:2; 26:14). Unless we are instructed otherwise in Scripture, we must assume that when "speaking in tongues" is mentioned elsewhere in Acts, or in 1 Corinthians, it refers to an identical experience: believers praising God in the Spirit in languages that are known.

Why did God do this? For one thing, Pentecost was a reversal of the judgment at the Tower of Babel when God confused man's language (Gen. 11:1–9). God's judgment at Babel scattered the people, but God's blessing at Pentecost united the believers in the Spirit. At Babel, the people were unable to understand each other, but at Pentecost, men heard God's praises and understood what was said. The Tower of Babel was a scheme designed to praise men and make a name for men, but Pentecost brought praise to God. The building of Babel was an act of rebellion, but Pentecost was a ministry of humble submission to God. What a contrast!

Another reason for this gift of tongues was to let the people know that the gospel was for the whole world. God wants to speak to every person in his or her own language and give the saving message of salvation in Jesus Christ. The emphasis in the book of Acts is on worldwide evangelization, "unto the uttermost part of the earth" (Acts 1:8). "The Spirit of Christ is the spirit of missions," said Henry Martyn, "and the nearer we get to Him, the more intensely missionary we must become."

Apparently the sound of the wind drew the people to the temple where the believers were gathered, but it was the praise by the believers that really captured their attention. The careless listeners mocked and accused the believers of being drunk, but others were sincerely concerned to find out what was going on. The people were perplexed (Acts 2:6), amazed (vv. 7, 12), and they marveled (v. 2:7).

It is interesting that the mockers should accuse the believers of being drunk, for wine is associated with the Holy Spirit (Eph. 5:18). Paul relates the two *in contrast,* for when a man is filled with strong drink, he loses control of himself and ends up being ashamed, but when a person is filled with the Spirit, he has self-control and glorifies God. Strong drink can bring a temporary exhilaration, but the Spirit gives a deep satisfaction and a lasting joy.

THE CHURCH WITNESSING TO THE LOST (2:14–41)

Peter did not preach in tongues; he addressed his audience in the everyday Aramaic that they understood. The message was given by a Jew, to Jews (Acts 2:14, 22, 29, 36), on a Jewish holy day, about the resurrection of the Jewish Messiah, whom their nation had crucified. The Gentiles who were there were proselytes to the Jewish religion (v. 10). Peter would not open the door of faith to the Gentiles until he visited Cornelius (Acts 10).

There are three explanations in Peter's sermon.

He explained what happened: The Spirit had come (vv. 14–21). The joyful worship of the believers was not the result of too much wine; it was the evidence of the arrival of God's Holy Spirit to dwell in His people. Orthodox Jews did not eat or drink before nine a.m. on the Sabbath or on a holy day, nor did they usually drink wine except with meals.

Peter did not say that Pentecost was the *fulfillment* of the prophecy of Joel 2:28–32, because the signs and wonders predicted had not occurred. When you read Joel's prophecy in context, you see that it deals with the nation of Israel in the end times, in connection with "the day of the Lord." However, Peter was led by the Spirit to see in the prophecy an application to the church. He said, "This is that same Holy Spirit that Joel wrote about. He is here!" Such an announcement would seem incredible to the Jews, because they thought God's Spirit was given only to a few select people (see Num. 11:28–29). But here were 120 of their fellow Jews, men and women, enjoying the blessing of the same Holy Spirit that had empowered Moses, David, and the prophets.

It was indeed the dawning of a new age, the "last days" in which God would bring to completion His plan of salvation for mankind. Jesus had finished the great work of redemption, and nothing more had to be done except to share the good news with the world, beginning with the nation of Israel. The invitation is, "Whosoever shall call on the name of the Lord shall be saved" (Acts 2:21).

He explained how it happened: Jesus was alive (vv. 22–35). News travels fast in the East, and probably most of the adults in Jerusalem, residents and visitors, knew about the arrest, trial, and crucifixion of Jesus of Nazareth. They also had heard rumors of an "official announcement" that His followers had stolen the body of Jesus just to make people think that He had kept His word and been raised from the dead.

But Peter told them the truth: Jesus of Nazareth had indeed been raised from the dead, and the resurrection proves that He is the Messiah! Peter gave them four proofs of the resurrection of Jesus Christ of Nazareth, and then he called on them to believe on Christ and be saved.

His first proof was the person of Jesus Christ (vv. 22–24). Peter's audience knew that Jesus was a real Person from the town of Nazareth and that He had performed many signs and miracles. (On "Jesus of Nazareth," see Acts 2:22; 3:6; 4:10; 6:14; 10:38; 22:8; 26:9; also 24:5.) It was clear that God's hand was on Him. They had heard Him speak and had watched His life. They had even seen Him raise the dead, yet they could find no fault in Him—and these things were not "done in a corner" (Acts 26:26)!

It was incredible that such a Man should be defeated by death. From one point of view, the crucifixion of Jesus was a terrible crime (Acts 2:23), but from another point of view it was a wonderful victory (v. 24). The word translated "pains" means "birth pangs," suggesting that the tomb was a "womb" out of which Jesus was "born" in resurrection glory (see Acts 13:33).

Peter's second proof was the prophecy of David (vv. 25–31). He quoted Psalm 16:8–11, verses that obviously could not apply to David, who was already dead and buried. Being a prophet of God, David wrote about the Messiah, that His soul would not remain in hades (the realm of the dead) or His body in the grave where it would decay.

The third proof was the witness of the believers (v. 33). After His resurrection, Jesus did not appear to the world at large, but to His own followers whom He had commissioned to give witness to others that He was alive (Acts 1:3, 22). But were these people dependable witnesses? Can we trust them? We certainly can! Prior to Christ's resurrection, the disciples did not even believe that He would be raised from the dead, and they themselves had to be convinced (Mark 16:9–14; Acts 1:3). They had nothing to gain by preaching a lie, because their message aroused official opposition and even led to the imprisonment and death of some of the believers. A few fanatics might be willing to believe and promote a lie for a time, but when thousands believe a message, and when that message is backed up by miracles, you cannot easily dismiss it. These witnesses were trustworthy.

Peter's fourth proof of the resurrection of Christ was the presence of the Holy Spirit (vv. 33–35). Follow his logic. If the Holy Spirit is in the world, then God must have sent Him. Joel promised that one day the Spirit would come, and Jesus Himself had promised to send the gift of the Holy Spirit to His people (Luke 24:49; John 14:26; 15:26; Acts 1:4). But if Jesus is dead, He cannot send the Spirit; therefore, He must be alive. Furthermore, He could not send the Spirit unless He had returned to heaven to the Father (John 16:7); so, Jesus has ascended to heaven! To back up this statement, Peter quoted Psalm 110:1, a verse that certainly could not be applied to David (note Matt. 22:41–46).

Peter's conclusion was both a declaration and an accusation: Jesus is your Messiah, *but you crucified Him* (see Acts 2:23)! Peter did not present the cross as the place where the sinless substitute died for the world, but where Israel killed her own Messiah! They committed the greatest crime in history! Was there any hope? Yes, for Peter gave a third explanation that was good news to their hearts.

He explained why it happened: to save sinners (vv. 36–41). The Holy Spirit took Peter's message and used it to convict the hearts of the listeners. (In Acts 5:33 and 7:54, a different Greek word is used that suggests anger rather than conviction for sin.) After all, if they were guilty of crucifying their Messiah, what might God do to them! Note that they addressed their question to the other apostles as well as to Peter, for all twelve were involved in the witness that day, and Peter was only first among equals.

Peter told them how to be saved: They had to repent of their sins and believe on Jesus Christ. They would give proof of the sincerity of their repentance and faith by being baptized in the name of Jesus Christ, thus identifying themselves publicly with their Messiah and Savior. Only by repenting and believing on Christ could they receive the gift of the Spirit (Gal. 3:2, 14), and this promise was for both the Jews and the "far off" Gentiles (Eph. 2:13–19).

It is unfortunate that the translation of Acts 2:38 in the King James Version suggests that people must be baptized in order to be saved, because this is not what the Bible teaches. The Greek word *eis* (which is translated "for" in the phrase "for the remission of sins") can mean "on account of or "on the basis of." In Matthew 3:11, John the Baptist baptized on the basis that people had repented. Acts 2:38 should not be used to teach salvation by baptism. If baptism is essential for salvation, it seems strange that Peter said nothing about baptism in his other sermons (Acts 3:12–26; 5:29–32; 10:34–43). In fact, the people in the home of Cornelius received the Holy Spirit *before they were baptized* (Acts 10:44–48)! Since believers are commanded to be baptized, it is important that we have a clean conscience by obeying (1 Peter 3:21), but we must not think that baptism is a part of salvation. If so, then nobody in Hebrews 11 was saved, because none of them was ever baptized.

Acts 2:40 indicates that the apostles continued to share the Word and to urge the people to trust Jesus Christ. They looked on the nation of Israel as a "crooked generation" that was under condemnation (Matt. 16:4; 17:17; Phil. 2:15). Actually, the nation would have about forty years before Rome would come and destroy the city and the temple and scatter the people. History was repeating itself. During the forty years in the wilderness, the new generation "saved itself" from the older generation that rebelled against God. Now, God would give His people another forty years of grace, and on that day, three thousand people repented, believed, and were saved.

THE CHURCH WALKING IN THE SPIRIT (2:42–47)

The believers continued to use the temple for their place of assembly and ministry, but they also met in various homes. The three thousand new converts needed instruction in the Word and fellowship with God's people if they were to grow and become effective witnesses. The early church did more than make converts; they also made *disciples* (Matt. 28:19–20).

Two phrases in Acts 2:42 may need explanation. "Breaking of bread" probably refers to their regular meals, but at the close of each meal, they probably paused to remember the Lord by observing what we call "the Lord's Supper." Bread and wine were the common fare at a Jewish table. The word *fellowship* means much more than "being together." It means "having in common" and probably refers to the sharing of material goods that was practiced in the early church. This was certainly not a form of modern communism, for the program was totally voluntary, temporary (Acts 11:27–30), and motivated by love.

The church was unified (Acts 2:44), magnified (v. 47a), and multiplied (v. 47b). It had a powerful testimony among the unsaved Jews, not only because of the miracles done by the apostles (v. 43), but also because of the way the members of the fellowship loved each other and served the Lord. The risen Lord continued to work with them (Mark 16:20), and people continued to be saved. What a church!

The Christians you meet in the book of Acts were not content to meet once a week for "services as usual." They met daily (Acts 2:46), cared daily (6:1), won souls daily (2:47), searched the Scriptures daily

(17:11), and increased in number daily (16:5). Their Christian faith was a day-to-day reality, not a once-a-week routine. Why? Because the risen Christ was a living reality to them, and His resurrection power was at work in their lives through the Spirit.

The promise is still good: "Whosoever shall call on the name of the Lord shall be saved" (Acts 2:21; Rom. 10:13). Have you called? Have you trusted Jesus Christ to save you?

QUESTIONS FOR PERSONAL REFLECTION
OR GROUP DISCUSSION

1. How do we define success in the church?

2. Compare your definition with the priorities of the first church as you read this chapter.

3. Read Acts 2:1–13. If you were a reporter in Jerusalem on Shavuot, or Pentecost, how would you have reported what happened?

4. Wiersbe says the book of Acts contains nonrepeatable events, transitional happenings, and basic spiritual principles. What examples of each of these do you see in Acts 2?

5. Read verses 14–41. How did Peter explain what was happening that day?

6. What proofs did Peter give of Christ's resurrection?

7. How can we use these same proofs when we witness?

8. Read verses 42–47. What are the primary characteristics of the first church?

9. How does your church compare with the first church? In what ways should it be more like the first church?

10. What can you do to help your church be more like what you've described?

Chapter Three

THE POWER OF HIS NAME

(Acts 3:1—4:4)

T he emphasis in Acts 3 and 4 is on the name of the Lord Jesus (Acts 3:6, 16; 4:7, 10, 12, 17–18, 30). A name, of course, implies much more than identification; it carries with it authority, reputation, and power. When somebody says, "You can use my name!" you sincerely hope the name is worth using. If an order is given in the name of the President of the United States or the Prime Minister of Great Britain, those who receive the order know that they are obligated to obey. If I were to issue orders at the White House or at No. 10 Downing Street (even if I could get in), nobody would pay much attention because my name has no official authority behind it.

But the name of the Lord Jesus has *all authority* behind it, for He is the Son of God (Matt. 28:18). Because His name is "above every name" (Phil. 2:9–11), He deserves our worship and obedience. The great concern of the first Christians was that the name of Jesus Christ, God's Son, be glorified, and believers today should have that same concern.

As we study this section, we should note that the Jewish emphasis is very pronounced. Peter addressed Jewish men (Acts 3:12) and called them "children of the prophets, and of the covenant" (v. 25). He referred to the

Jewish fathers (v. 13) as well as to the prophets (vv. 18, 21–25). The phrase "times of restitution" (v. 21) is definitely Jewish and refers to the messianic kingdom promised in the prophets. The message is still going out "to the Jew first" (Rom 1:16) and is presented in Jewish terms.

There are three stages in this event, and each stage reveals something wonderful about Jesus Christ.

1. AMAZEMENT: JESUS THE HEALER (3:1–10)

The believers were still attached to the temple and to the traditional hours of prayer (Ps. 55:17; Dan. 6:10; Acts 10:30). Keep in mind that Acts 1—10 describes a gradual transition from Israel to the Gentiles and from "Jewish Christianity" (note Acts 21:20) to the "one body" made up of both Jews and Gentiles. It took several years before many of the Jewish believers really understood the place of the Gentiles in God's program, and this understanding did not come without its conflicts.

The contrast between Acts 2 and 3 is interesting: Peter the preacher—Peter the personal worker; multitudes—one poor man; ministry resulting in blessing—ministry resulting in arrest and persecution. The events in Acts 3 are an illustration of the last phrase in Acts 2:47, showing us how the Lord added to His church daily. While the Holy Spirit is not named in this chapter, He was certainly at work in and through the apostles, performing His ministry of glorifying Jesus Christ (John 16:14).

Peter and John are often found together in Scripture. They were partners in the fishing business (Luke 5:10); they prepared the last Passover for Jesus (Luke 22:8); they ran to the tomb on the first Easter Sunday morning (John 20:3–4); and they ministered to the Samaritans who believed on Jesus Christ (Acts 8:14). Now that they were filled with the Holy Spirit, the apostles were no longer competing for greatness, but were at last working faithfully together to build the church (Ps. 133).

That Peter noticed the lame beggar is another evidence of the Spirit's ministry. No doubt thousands of people were near the temple (Acts 4:4), and perhaps scores of beggars, but the Lord told Peter to heal a lame man lying at the Beautiful Gate. There were nine gates that led from the court of the Gentiles into the temple itself. Scholars are not agreed, but the Beautiful Gate was probably the "Eastern Gate" that led into the court of the women. Made of Corinthian bronze, the gate looked like gold, and it certainly was a choice place for a lame man to beg.

The giving of alms was an important part of the Jewish faith, so beggars found it profitable to be near the temple. Since the believers had pooled their resources (Acts 2:44–45), the two apostles had no money to give, but money was not what the man needed most. He needed salvation for his soul and healing for his body, and money could provide neither. Through the power of the name of Jesus, the beggar was completely healed, and he was so happy and excited that he acted like a child, leaping and praising God.

It is easy to see in this man an illustration of what salvation is like. He was born lame, and all of us are born unable to walk so as to please God. Our father Adam had a fall and passed his lameness on to all of his descendants (Rom. 5:12–21). The man was also poor, and we as sinners are bankrupt before God, unable to pay the tremendous debt that we owe Him (Luke 7:36–50). He was "outside the temple," and all sinners are separated from God, no matter how near to the door they might be. The man was healed wholly by the grace of God (Eph. 2:8–9), and the healing was immediate (Acts 3:7). He gave evidence of what God had done by "walking, and leaping, and praising God" (v. 8) and by publicly identifying himself with the apostles, both in the temple (v. 11) and in their arrest (4:14). Now that he could stand, there was no question *where* this man stood!

2. INDICTMENT: JESUS, THE SON OF GOD (3:11–16)

The healing of the lame beggar drew a crowd around the three men. Solomon's Porch, on the east side of the temple, was a corridor where our Lord had ministered (John 10:23) and where the church worshipped (Acts 5:12).

In his sermon at Pentecost, Peter had to refute the accusation that the believers were drunk. In this sermon, he had to refute the notion that he and John had healed the man by their own power. (Paul and Barnabas would face a similar situation after healing a lame man. See Acts 14:8–18.) Peter immediately identified the source of the miracle— Jesus Christ, the Son of God. Wisely, Peter said that this was the God of their fathers, the God of Abraham, Isaac, and Jacob.

The Spirit certainly gave Peter boldness as he reminded the Jews of the way they had treated Jesus. They had denied Him and delivered Him up to be crucified. Even worse, they had asked for a guilty man, Barabbas, to be set free so that an innocent prisoner might be crucified! In order to convince them of their crimes, Peter used several different names and titles for our Lord: God's Son, Jesus, the Holy One, the Just One, the Prince (Pioneer) of life. This was no ordinary man that they had handed over to the Romans to crucify!

Calvary may have been man's last word, but the empty tomb was God's last word. He glorified His Son by raising Him from the dead and taking Him back to heaven. The enthroned Christ had sent His Holy Spirit and was working through His church. The healed beggar was proof that Jesus was alive. If ever a people were guilty, it was the people Peter addressed in the temple. They were guilty of killing their own Messiah!

This is probably not the kind of message we would give at an evangelistic meeting today, because it was designed especially for Peter's Jewish audience. As at Pentecost, Peter was addressing people who knew the Scriptures and were acquainted with the recent events in Jerusalem (see Luke 24:18). It was not a group of ignorant pagans with no religious background. Furthermore, the Jewish leaders had indeed perpetrated a great injustice when they arrested and condemned Jesus and asked Pilate to have

Him crucified. How many citizens agreed with their decision, we do not know, but you can imagine the remorse of the people when they learned that they had betrayed and killed their own Messiah.

There must be conviction before a sinner can experience conversion. Unless a patient is convinced that he is sick, he will never accept the diagnosis or take the treatment. Peter turned the temple into a courtroom and laid all the evidence out for everybody to see. How could two ordinary fishermen perform such a great miracle unless God was with them? Nobody would dare deny the miracle because the beggar stood there before them all in "perfect soundness" (Acts 3:16; 4:14). To accept the miracle would have been to admit that Jesus Christ is indeed the living Son of God and that His name has power.

3. ENCOURAGEMENT: JESUS, THE SAVIOR (3:17—4:4)

But Peter did not leave the people without hope. In fact, he almost seemed to defend them by pointing out that they had acted in ignorance (Acts 3:17) while at the same time they had fulfilled the Word of God (v. 18).

In the Old Testament law, there is a difference between deliberate sins and sins of ignorance (see Lev. 4—5; Num. 15:22–31). The person who sinned presumptuously was a rebel against God and was guilty of great sin. He was to be "cut off" from his people (Num. 15:30–31), which could mean excommunication and even death. The defiant "high-handed" sinner was condemned, but the person who sinned unwittingly and without deliberate intent was given opportunity to repent and seek God's forgiveness. Ignorance does not remove the sinner's guilt, but it does mitigate the circumstances.

Jesus had prayed, "Father, forgive them; for they know not what they do" (Luke 23:34), and God had answered that prayer. Instead of sending judgment, He sent the Holy Spirit to empower His church and to convict lost sinners. Israel's situation was something like that of the "manslayer" who killed his neighbor without prior malicious intent, and fled to the nearest city of refuge (Num. 35:9–34). So long as he remained in the city, he was safe, for then the avengers could not reach him and kill him. He was free to go home only after the death of the high priest. Peter invited these "murderers" to flee by faith to Jesus Christ and find refuge in Him (Heb. 6:18).

In his previous sermon, Peter had explained that the cross was the meeting place of divine sovereignty and human responsibility (Acts 2:23), and he repeated this truth in this second sermon (3:17–18). There are mysteries here that the human mind cannot fully understand, so we must accept them by faith. God had a plan from all eternity, yet His plan did not force men to act against their own will. The prophets had foretold the sufferings and death of the Messiah, and the nation fulfilled these prophecies without realizing what they were doing. When God cannot rule, He overrules and always accomplishes His divine purposes and decrees.

Having announced the crime, presented the evidence, and explained the nature of their sin, Peter then offered them pardon (Acts 3:19–26)! What a strange thing for the prosecuting attorney to become the defense attorney and the pardoning judge! Peter's burden was to encourage his people to trust Christ and experience His gracious salvation.

What did he tell them to do? First of all, *they had to repent of their sins* (see Acts 2:38; 5:31; 17:30), which means to have a change of mind about themselves, their sin, and Jesus Christ. Repentance is much more than "feeling sorry for your sins." As the little Sunday school girl said, "It means feeling sorry enough to quit!" False sorrow for sin could be mere regret ("I'm sorry I got caught!") or remorse ("I feel terrible!"), and such feelings have a tendency to pass away. Repentance is not the same as "doing penance," as though we have to make a special sacrifice to God to prove that we are sincere. True repentance is admitting that what God says is true, and because it is true, to change our minds about our sins and about the Savior.

The message of repentance was not new to the Jews, for John the Baptist had preached it and so had Jesus (Matt. 3:2; 4:17). In one sense, repentance is a gift from God (Acts 11:18); in another sense, it is the heart's response to the convicting ministry of the Spirit of God (26:20). The person who sincerely repents will have little problem putting his faith in the Savior.

Second, they had to *be converted,* "to turn again," and exercise saving faith in Jesus Christ. The biblical message is "repentance toward God, and faith toward our Lord Jesus Christ" (Acts 20:21), and the two go together. Unless we turn from our sins, we cannot put saving faith in Jesus Christ. It is unfortunate that some preachers have so ignored the doctrine of repentance that their "converts" lack a true sense of conviction of sin. Balanced evangelism presents to the sinner both repentance and faith.

Peter announced what would happen if they repented and turned to Jesus Christ: "in order that your sins may be blotted out, in order that the times of refreshing may come from the presence of the Lord, in order that He may send Jesus Christ" (literal translation). There was a promise for the individual (sins forgiven) and a promise for the nation (times of spiritual refreshing). Peter was actually calling for *national repentance,* for the nation through its leaders had denied its Messiah and condemned Him to die. The declaration is that, if the nation repented and believed, the Messiah would return and establish the promised kingdom. The nation did not repent—and certainly God knew this would happen—so the message eventually moved from the Jews to the Samaritans (Acts 8) and to the Gentiles (Acts 10).

The emphasis in Acts 3:22–25 is on *the prophets* who had announced the coming of the Messiah. Peter quoted from Moses (Deut. 18:15, 18–19) and reminded his listeners that Moses had predicted the arrival of a prophet, and this prophet was the Messiah (see Luke 24:19; John 1:19–28; 6:14). Not to obey ("hear") this prophet meant condemnation. But Moses was not the only one who foretold the coming of Jesus Christ, for all the prophets united in their witness to Him (see Luke 24:25–27, 44–48).

When Peter spoke about "these days," to what "days" was he referring? The days of the life and ministry of Jesus Christ, the days when God's prophet would speak to His people and offer them salvation. The nation's rejection of Him made them especially guilty because the Jews were the privileged "sons of the prophets and of the covenant." They had sinned against a flood of light!

When God called Abraham, He made an unconditional covenant with him and his descendants that through them the nations of the world would be blessed (Gen. 12:1–3). This promise was fulfilled when Jesus Christ came into the world through the Jewish nation (Gal. 3:6–14). The gospel message came "to the Jew first" because the Jews were God's chosen instrument through whom the Gentiles would be blessed (Acts 3:26; 13:46; Rom. 1:16). The first Christians were Jews, and the first missionaries were Jews.

But notice that Peter did not permit the "national blessings" to overshadow the personal responsibility of the individuals listening to his message (Acts 3:26). God raised up Jesus Christ and sent Him to *each one* who would turn away from his iniquities (note v. 20). National repentance depends on personal repentance, the response of individual sinners to the message of salvation. Peter was addressing a large crowd, but he still made the application personal.

His message produced two opposite results: (1) some two thousand Jews believed the Word and were converted, and (2) the religious leaders of the nation rejected the message and tried to silence the apostles. We have here the beginning of the persecution about which Jesus had already warned His followers (Matt. 10:17–18; Luke 21:12–15; John 15:18—16:4).

We would expect the Sadducees to oppose the message because they did not believe in the resurrection of the human body (Acts 23:6–8). Peter's fearless declaration that Jesus Christ had been raised from the dead ran contrary to their religious beliefs. If the common people questioned the theology of their spiritual leaders, it could undermine the authority of the whole Jewish council. Instead of honestly examining the evidence, the leaders arrested the apostles and kept them in custody overnight, intending to try them the next day. However, the arrival of the temple guards could not prevent two thousand men from trusting Jesus Christ and identifying themselves with the believers in Jerusalem.

As you review this section of Acts, you cannot help but be impressed with some practical truths that should encourage all of us in our witnessing for Christ.

1. God is long-suffering with lost sinners. The leaders of Israel had rejected the ministry of John the Baptist (Matt. 21:23–27) and the ministry of Jesus, and yet God gave them another opportunity to repent and be saved. They had denied and slain their own Messiah, and yet God patiently held back His judgment and sent His Spirit to deal with them. God's people today need patience as we witness to a lost world.

2. True witness involves the "bad news" of sin and guilt as well as the "good news" of salvation through faith in Jesus Christ. There can be no true faith in Christ unless first there is repentance from sin. It is the ministry of the Holy Spirit to convict lost sinners (John 16:7–11), and He will do this if we faithfully witness and use God's Word.

3. The way to reach the masses is by helping the individual sinner. Peter and John won the crippled beggar, and his transformed life led to the conversion of two thousand men! The servant of God who has no time for personal work with individual sinners will not be given many

opportunities for ministering to great crowds. Like Jesus, the apostles took time for individuals.

4. The best defense of the truth of the Christian faith is a changed life. The healed beggar was "exhibit A" in Peter's defense of the resurrection of Jesus Christ. In his evangelistic ministries, the Methodist preacher Samuel Chadwick used to pray for "a Lazarus" in every campaign, some "great sinner" whose conversion would shock the community. He got the idea from John 12:9–11. God answered his prayers in meeting after meeting as infamous wicked men trusted Christ and became witnesses through their changed lives. Let's go after the "hard cases" and see what God can do!

5. Whenever God blesses, Satan shows up to oppose the work and silence the witness, and often he uses religious people to do his work. The same crowd that opposed the ministry of Jesus Christ also opposed the work of the apostles, and they will oppose our ministry today. Expect it—but don't let it stop you! The important thing is not that we are comfortable, but that the name of the Lord is glorified through the preaching of the gospel.

6. God has promised to bless and use His Word, so let's be faithful to witness. Jesus even prayed that our witness would have success (John 17:20), so we have every reason to be encouraged. There is power in the name of Jesus, so we need not fear to witness and call sinners to repent.

7. The name of Jesus Christ still has power! While we may not perform the same apostolic miracles today that were seen in the early church, we can still claim the authority of Jesus Christ as He has instructed us in the Word.

We can preach the "remission of sins" in His name (Luke 24:47) so that people might believe and have "life through his name" (John 20:31). We can give someone a cup of cold water in His name (Mark 9:41), and we can receive a child in His name (Matt. 18:5). These ministries may not seem as spectacular as healing a cripple, but they are still important to the work of God.

We can ask in His name as we pray (John 14:13–14; 15:16; 16:23–26). When we ask the Father for something "in the name of Jesus Christ," it is as though Jesus Himself were asking it. If we remember this, it will help to keep us from asking for things unworthy of His name.

Yes, the name of Jesus Christ still has authority and power. Let's go forth in His name and conquer!

QUESTIONS FOR PERSONAL REFLECTION OR GROUP DISCUSSION

1. Who are some people whose names/positions are synonymous with authority? Why?

2. Read Acts 3:1–10. What is the difference between Jesus' authority and the apostles' authority?

3. How is the lame beggar in this passage an illustration of what salvation is like?

4. Read Acts 3:11–26. What do you learn from Peter's sermon that can help you witness?

5. How are both repentance and conversion necessary for salvation?

6. Read Acts 4:1–4. How did people respond to Peter's sermon? Why?

7. What have you learned from this passage to encourage you as you witness to others?

8. What does it mean to live in the power of the Holy Spirit today, so that people don't just hear our words about Christ but see God acting through us?

9. What would it take for you to live as a witness for Christ in the power of the Holy Spirit this week?

Chapter Four

PERSECUTION, PRAYER, AND POWER

(Acts 4:5–31)

The early church had none of the "advantages" that some ministries boast of and depend on today. They did not have big budgets provided by wealthy donors. Their pastors lacked credentials from the accepted schools, nor did they have the endorsement of the influential political leaders of that day. Most of their ministers had jail records and would probably have a hard time today *joining* our churches, let alone *leading* them. What really was the secret of their success? This chapter provides the answer: The Christians of the early church knew how to pray so that God's hand could work in mighty power.

When asked to explain the secret of his remarkable ministry, the noted British preacher Charles Haddon Spurgeon replied, "My people pray for me." St. Augustine said, "Pray as though everything depended on God, and work as though everything depended on you." Prayer is not an escape from responsibility; it is our *response* to God's *ability*. True prayer energizes us for service and battle.

Once again, the focus of attention is on the name of the Lord Jesus Christ (Acts 4:7, 10, 12, 17–18). In this chapter, we see what three groups of people do with His name.

1. THE APOSTLES: DEFENDING HIS NAME (4:5–14)

The court (vv. 5–7). The court was essentially composed of the high priest's family. The Jewish religious system had become so corrupt that the offices were passed from one relative to another without regard for the Word of God. When Annas was deposed from the priesthood, Caiaphas, his son-in-law, was appointed. In fact, five of Annas's sons held the office at one time or another. Somebody has defined a "nepotist" as "a man who, being evil, knows how to give good gifts to his children." Annas certainly qualified.

This was an official meeting of the Sanhedrin (Acts 4:15), the same council that a few months before had condemned Jesus to die. In fact, these officials recognized Peter and John as the associates of Jesus (Acts 4:13). The Sanhedrin was charged with the responsibility of protecting the Jewish faith, and this meant that they had to examine every new teacher and teaching that appeared in the land (see Deut. 13). They certainly had the right to investigate what the church was doing, but they did not have the right to arrest innocent men and then refuse to honestly examine the evidence.

Their question was legal, but they did everything they could to avoid admitting that a miracle had taken place (Acts 4:14). They were evasive and merely referred to the miracle as "this." They were probably scornful as well, so that their question might be paraphrased, "Where did common people like you get the power and authority to do a thing like this?" It was once again the question of "By whose name?" After all, the apostles might be in league with the Devil! Even Satan can perform miracles!

The case (vv. 8–14). Peter spoke in the power of the Holy Spirit of God. Note that Peter was again filled with the Spirit (see Acts 2:4) and would experience another filling before the day ended (Acts 4:31). There is one baptism of the Spirit, and this is at conversion (1 Cor. 12:13), but there must be many fillings of the Spirit if the believer is to be an effective witness for Jesus Christ (Eph. 5:18ff.).

Peter respectfully began with an explanation of how the miracle occurred. Certainly the members of the Sanhedrin had seen the crippled beggar many times, and perhaps they had even given alms to him and piously prayed for him. How was this well-known man healed? "By the name of Jesus Christ of Nazareth!" Those words must have pierced the hearts of the members of the council! They thought they had finished with the prophet from Nazareth, and now His followers were telling everybody that Jesus was alive! Since the Sadducees did not believe in the resurrection of the dead, Peter's statement was almost a declaration of war!

But the Spirit was telling Peter what to say (see Luke 21:12–15), and the apostle quoted Psalm 118:22, definitely a messianic reference (see Matt. 21:42; 1 Peter 2:4–8). He made it clear that the members of the council were "the builders" and that they had rejected God's Stone, Jesus, the Son of God.

The image of "the stone" was not new to these men who were experts in the Old Testament Scriptures. They knew that the "Rock" was a symbol of God (Deut. 32:4, 15, 18, 31; 2 Sam. 22:2; Ps. 18:2; Isa. 28:16), and that the prophet Daniel had used the rock to picture Messiah and the coming of His kingdom on earth (Dan. 2:31–45). The Jews stumbled over the Rock (Rom. 9:32; 1 Cor. 1:23) and rejected Him, just as Psalm 118:22 had predicted. However, to those who have trusted Him, Jesus Christ is the precious Cornerstone (1 Peter 2:4–8) and the chief Cornerstone (Eph. 2:20).

Peter went on to explain that Jesus is not only the Stone, but He is also the Savior (Acts 4:12). Peter saw in the healing of the beggar a picture of the spiritual healing that comes in salvation. "Made whole" in Acts 4:9 is a translation of the same Greek word that is translated "saved" in Acts 4:12, for salvation means wholeness and spiritual health. Jesus Christ is the Great

Physician who alone can heal mankind's greatest malady, the sickness of sin (Mark 2:14–17). Of course, Peter also had "all the people of Israel" in mind as he spoke (see Acts 4:10) because the message was still going out exclusively to the Jews. Even Psalm 118, from which Peter quoted, speaks of a future national salvation for Israel.

2. The Council: Opposing His Name (4:15–22)

Their problem (vv. 13–14). They were in a dilemma; no matter which way they turned, they were "trapped." They could not deny the miracle because the man was standing before them, and yet they could not explain how "uneducated and untrained men" (NASB) could perform such a mighty deed. Peter and John were ordinary fishermen, not professional scribes or authorized ministers of the Jewish religion. They were disciples of Jesus of Nazareth, but—He was dead! The council took notice of the courage and confidence of Peter and John, as well as the power of Peter's words, and it all added up to perplexity.

It is important to note that, of itself, the miracle was not proof of the resurrection of Christ or even of the truth of Peter's message. Satan can perform miracles (2 Thess. 2:9–10) and false prophets can do wonders (Deut. 13:1–5). The miracle and the message, *in the context of all that had been going on since Pentecost,* was one more evidence that Jesus Christ was alive and at work in the church by His Holy Spirit. In both sermons, Peter used the Old Testament to support and explain his claims, and this is one evidence of a true prophet of God (Deut. 13:1–5; Isa. 8:20). Miracles are not a substitute for the Word of God (Luke 16:27–31).

Their deliberation (vv. 15–18). The council did not seek for truth, but rather sought for some way to avoid the truth! Had they honestly considered the evidence and meekly listened to the message, they might have been saved, but their pride and hardness of heart stood in the way. Some of the chief priests and elders had experienced a similar dilemma during

Passover when they had tried to trap Jesus in the temple (Matt. 21:23–27). Some people never learn! But their response is proof that miracles alone can never convict or convert the lost sinner. Only the Word of God can do that (see John 11:45–53; Acts 14:1–20).

Their conclusion. They wanted to "let the thing die a natural death." This meant threatening the apostles and forbidding them to teach and preach in the name of Jesus. This official sentence shows how much the enemy fears the witness of the church, for Satan has been trying to silence God's people from the very beginning. Sad to say, he has succeeded with far too many Christians, the "silent witnesses" of the church. Even the existential philosopher Albert Camus said, "What the world expects of Christians is that Christians should speak out, loud and clear … in such a way that never a doubt, never the slightest doubt, could arise in the heart of the simplest man."

The council did not want the gospel message to spread, and yet that is exactly what happened! From 120 praying men and women in Acts 1, the church increased to more than three thousand on the day of Pentecost, and now there were more than five thousand disciples in the fellowship. In the days that followed, "believers were the more added to the Lord, multitudes both of men and women" (Acts 5:14; and see 6:1, 7). Satan's attempts to silence the church only led to a stronger witness for the Lord.

The failure of the council (vv. 19–22). This was evident when Peter refused to be intimidated by their threats. All of us need to follow Peter's example and make our decisions on the basis of "Is it right?" and not "Is it popular?" or "Is it safe?" However, we must be sure that we have the clear teaching of the Word of God on our side before we take a stand against the authority of the government. Peter knew what the Lord had commanded the believers to do (Acts 1:8), and he was going to obey Him at any cost.

It is popular today to promote various causes by defying the government, disobeying the law, and defending these actions on the basis of conscience. Since even some Christians are involved in this approach to social action, it is important to understand the kind of "civil disobedience" practiced by people in the Bible. Peter and John are not the only ones who disobeyed the authorities in order to serve God. A list of "dedicated conscientious objectors" would include, among others, the Jewish midwives (Ex. 1), Moses' parents (Heb. 11:23), Daniel (Dan. 1; 6), and the three Hebrew children (Dan. 3). When you examine the records, you discover the biblical principles by which they operated, principles that are not always followed today.

To begin with, each of these "objectors" had a message from God that could not be questioned. The midwives and Moses' parents knew that it was wrong to murder the babies. Daniel and his friends, and the three Hebrew men, knew that it was wrong to eat food offered to idols or to bow down to idols in worship. Peter and John knew that they were under orders from their Master to preach the gospel to the ends of the earth, and that it would be wrong to obey the Sanhedrin. All of these people were faithfully obeying a clear word from God and not just following some selfish personal whim of their own.

Second, their convictions touched every area of their lives, In other words, they did everything with "conscience toward God" (1 Peter 2:19) because they belonged to God. The university student today whose conscience permits him to cheat on exams or drive while drunk, but not register for military service, does not convince me that he is really cultivating a healthy conscience. When a person's *total life* is under the direction of a godly conscience, then I find it easier to have confidence in his unpopular decisions.

Note also that our examples from the Bible acted with respect and courtesy, even when they defied the law. It is possible for Christians to respect authority and at the same time disobey the authorities (see Rom. 13; Titus 3:1–2; 1 Peter 2:13–25). Daniel tried to avoid getting his guard into trouble, and the apostles used their arrests as opportunities for witness. This is quite a contrast to some of the modern "Christian objectors" who seem to major on denunciation and accusation rather than loving witness.

Of course, the greatest example of unjust suffering is that of Jesus Christ, and we must imitate Him (see 1 Peter 2:13–25). Jesus teaches us that righteous protest against injustice always involves sacrifice and suffering, and must be motivated by love. God's people must be careful not to clothe their prejudice in the garments of "righteous indignation" and pass themselves off as courageous soldiers of conscience. We must examine our own hearts honestly to make certain we are not conducting a "holy war" just to satisfy inner frustrations.

Because they had no real case to offer, the council could only threaten the men and let them go. After all, when you have a living miracle before you, as well as an approving public around you, you must be careful what you do!

3. The Church: Calling on His Name (4:23–31)

The greatest concentration of power in Jerusalem that day was in the prayer meeting that followed the trial. This is one of the truly great prayers recorded in the Bible, and it is a good example for us to follow.

To begin with, it was a prayer that was born out of witness and service for the Lord. Peter and John had just come in "from the trenches," and the church met to pray in order to defeat the enemy. Too often today, believers gather for prayer as though attending a concert or a party. There is little sense of urgency and danger because most of us are comfortable in our Christian walk. If more of God's people were witnessing for Christ in daily life, there would be more urgency and blessing when the church meets for prayer.

It was a united prayer meeting as they "lifted up their voice to God with one accord" (Acts 4:24; see 1:14). The people were of one heart and mind, and God was pleased to answer their requests. Division in the church always hinders prayer and robs the church of spiritual power.

Their praying was based solidly on the Word of God, in this case, Psalm 2. The Word of God and prayer must always go together (John 15:7). In His Word, God speaks to us and tells us what He wants to do. In prayer, we speak to Him and make ourselves available to accomplish His will. True prayer is not telling God what to do, but asking God to do His will in us and through us (1 John 5:14–15). It means getting God's will done on earth, not man's will done in heaven.

They did not pray to have their circumstances changed or their enemies put out of office. Rather, they asked God to empower them to make the best use of their circumstances and to accomplish what He had already determined (Acts 4:28). This was not "fatalism" but faith in the Lord of history who has a perfect plan and is always victorious. They asked for divine enablement, not escape, and God gave them the power that they needed.

"Do not pray for easy lives," wrote Phillips Brooks. "Pray to be stronger men and women. Do not pray for tasks equal to your powers. Pray for powers equal to your tasks." That is the way the early Christians prayed, and that is the way God's people should pray today.

They addressed God as "Sovereign Lord," the God who is in control of all things. The Greek word gives us our English word *despot,* a ruler who exercises absolute power, either benevolently or abusively. Simeon used this same title when he prayed in the temple (Luke 2:29). It is good to know the Sovereign Lord when you are experiencing persecution.

They also approached Him as the Creator, for, after all, if your Father is "Lord of heaven and earth," what have you to fear (see Matt. 11:25–30)? Nehemiah approached God on this same basis (Neh. 9:6), and so did the psalmist (see Ps. 145) and the prophet Isaiah (Isa. 42). Years later, when he wrote his first epistle, Peter encouraged suffering saints to yield themselves to the faithful Creator (1 Peter 4:19).

Psalm 2 describes the revolt of the nations against the Lord and His Christ. The psalm originally grew out of the crowning of a new king in Israel, perhaps David, but its ultimate message points to the King of Kings, Jesus Christ. Whenever a new king was enthroned, the vassal rulers around were required to come and submit to him, but some of them refused to do this. God only laughed at their revolt, for He knew that they could never stand up against His King.

The early believers applied the message of this psalm to their own situation and identified their adversaries as Herod, Pilate, the Romans, and the Jews. These enemies had "ganged up" against Jesus Christ and even crucified Him, yet God raised Him from the dead and enthroned Him in heaven. All of this was a part of God's perfect plan (see Acts 2:23; 3:18), so there was no need to fear.

The early church strongly believed in God's sovereignty and His perfect plan for His people. But note that they did not permit their faith in divine sovereignty to destroy human responsibility, for they were faithful to witness and pray. It is when God's people get out of balance and overemphasize either sovereignty or responsibility that the church loses power. Again, we are reminded of Augustine's wise words, "Pray as though everything depends on God, and work as though everything depended on you." Faith in a sovereign Lord is a tremendous encouragement for God's people to keep serving the Lord when the going is difficult.

They did not ask for protection; they asked for power. They did not ask for fire from heaven to destroy the enemy (see Luke 9:51–56) but for power from heaven to preach the Word and heal the sick (see Matt. 5:10–12, 43–48). Their great desire was for boldness in the face of opposition (see Acts 4:17). The emphasis is on the hand of God at work in the life of the church (Acts 4:28, 30), not the hand of man at work for God.

Believing prayer releases God's power and enables God's hand to move (Isa. 50:2; 64:1–8).

Finally, note that they wanted to glorify God's Child (Servant) Jesus Christ (Acts 4:27, 30). It was His name that gave them power to minister the Word and to perform miracles, and His name alone deserved the glory. The glory of God, not the needs of men, is the highest purpose of answered prayer.

God's answer was to shake the place where they were meeting and to fill the people once again with the Spirit of God (Acts 4:31). This gave them the boldness that they needed to continue to serve God in spite of official opposition. This was not a "second Pentecost" because there cannot be another Pentecost any more than there can be another Calvary. It was a new filling of the Spirit to equip the believers to serve the Lord and minister to the people.

We will consider Acts 4:32–37 in our next study, but it is worth noting that the new fullness of the Spirit also created a deeper unity among the people (Acts 4:34) and a greater desire to sacrifice and share with one another. They enjoyed "great power" and "great grace," which ought to be the marks of a "great" church. This led to a great ingathering of souls for the Lord.

"Lord, thou art God!" What a declaration of faith and what a practical application of good theology! However, if their lives had not been submitted to His control, they could not have prayed that way. Boldness in prayer is the result of faithfulness in life and service. The sovereignty of God is not an abstract doctrine that we accept and defend. It is a living truth that we act on and depend on for every need. When you are loyal to the Lord and put Him first (Acts 4:19), then you can trust Him to be faithful to you and see you through.

The name of Jesus Christ has not lost its power, but many of God's people have lost their power because they have stopped praying to the sovereign God. "Nothing lies beyond the reach of prayer except that which lies outside the will of God." I don't know who first said that, but the statement is absolutely true. Dr. R. A. Torrey, the noted evangelist and educator, said, "Pray for great things, expect great things, work for great things, but above all—pray."

The early church prayed, and God answered in mighty power.

QUESTIONS FOR PERSONAL REFLECTION
OR GROUP DISCUSSION

1. When things get tough, who and what helps you get through the situation? In what ways?

2. Read Acts 4:5–31. What tough situation were Peter and John in?

3. Why were the religious leaders so upset with Peter's preaching?

4. How did Peter and John respond to the leaders' command? Why?

5. What do you learn about civil disobedience from their response?

6. How did the Holy Spirit aid believers in remaining steadfast in the face of persecution?

7. What effect did John's and Peter's presence have on each other?

8. What do you learn about prayer and God from the believers' prayer in verses 24–30?

9. Do you have the kind of boldness to speak for Christ that Peter and John had? If so, how did you get it? If not, is that a problem? Please explain.

10. To whom can you witness this week? When will you try to do so?

Chapter Five

BEWARE OF THE SERPENT!

(Acts 4:32—5:16)

S atan had failed completely in his attempt to silence the witness of the church. However, the enemy never gives up; he simply changes his strategy. His first approach had been to attack the church from the outside, hoping that arrest and threats would frighten the leaders. When that failed, Satan decided to attack the church *from the inside* and use people who were a part of the fellowship.

We must face the fact that Satan is a clever foe. If he does not succeed as the devouring lion (1 Peter 5:8), then he attacks again as the deceiving serpent or an "angel of light" (2 Cor. 11:3, 13–14). Satan is both a murderer and a liar (John 8:44), and the church must be prepared for both attacks.

THE GENEROSITY OF THE BELIEVERS (4:32–37)

The believers had prayed and God's Spirit had filled them and given them new power. The church that depends on believing prayer will know the blessing of the Holy Spirit in its ministry. How can we tell when a local church is really filled with the Spirit? When you go back to the record of the first filling at Pentecost (Acts 2:44–47), you discover three outstanding characteristics of a Spirit-filled church.

(1) It is unified (2:44, 46). This is a God-given spiritual unity, not a man-made organizational uniformity. The church is an organism that is held together by life, and that life comes through the Holy Spirit. Of course, the church must be organized, for if an organism is not organized, it will die. However, when the organization starts to hinder spiritual life and ministry, then the church becomes just another religious institution that exists to keep itself going. When the Holy Spirit is at work, God's people will be united in their doctrinal beliefs, as well as in fellowship, giving, and worship (Acts 2:42).

(2) A Spirit-filled church is magnified and will have "favor with all the people" (2:47). In spite of the opposition of the rulers, the common people were drawn to the believers because something new and exciting was happening. When the religious leaders tried to silence the church, it was their fear of the people that restrained them (Acts 4:21; 5:26). Yes, a Spirit-filled church will have its enemies, but what the Lord is doing will attract the attention and the admiration of people who are hungry to know God.

(3) A Spirit-filled church is multiplied because the Lord will daily add new believers to the church (2:47). Evangelism will not be the work of a chosen few, but the daily delight and ministry of the whole congregation. In the early church, each member sought to be an effective witness for Jesus Christ, no matter where he happened to be. No wonder the church grew from 120 to over five thousand in just a short time!

How did Satan's attack affect the spiritual condition of the church? It had no effect at all! The fact that Peter and John were arrested, tried, and threatened had absolutely no effect on the spiritual life of the church, for the church was still unified (Acts 4:32), magnified (v. 33), and multiplied (v. 32)!

One evidence of the unity of the church was the way they sacrificed and shared with one another. When the Holy Spirit is at work, giving is a blessing and not a burden. We must keep in mind that this "Christian communism" was very unlike the political Communism of our day. What the believers did was purely voluntary (Acts 5:4) and was motivated by love. No doubt many of the new believers were visitors in Jerusalem, having come for the feasts, and they had to depend on their Christian friends to help meet their daily needs.

Nor should we think that every believer sold all his goods and brought the money to the apostles. Acts 4:34 indicates that some of the members from time to time sold various pieces of property and donated to the common treasury. When the assembly had a need, the Spirit directed someone to sell something and meet the need.

While the early church's spirit of sacrifice and loving generosity is worthy of our emulation, believers today are not required to imitate these practices. The principles of Christian giving are outlined in the Epistles, especially in 2 Corinthians 8—9, and nowhere are we instructed to bring our money and lay it at the pastor's feet (Acts 4:35) as though he were an apostle. It is the *spirit* of their giving that is important to us today and not the "letter" of their system.

Joseph, nicknamed "Barnabas" (son of encouragement), is introduced at this point for several reasons. First, he was a generous giver and illustrated the very thing Dr. Luke was describing. Second, his noble act apparently filled Ananias and Sapphira with envy so that they attempted to impress the church with their giving and ended up being killed. Third, Barnabas had a most important ministry in the church and is mentioned at least twenty-five times in the book of Acts and another five times in the Epistles. In fact, it is Barnabas who encouraged Paul in his early service for the Lord (Acts 9:26–27; 11:19–30; 13:1–5) and who gave his cousin John Mark the encouragement he needed after his failure (Acts 13:13; 15:36–41; Col. 4:10).

Levites were not permitted to own land, so it is difficult to understand how Barnabas acquired the property that he sold. Perhaps that particular law (Num. 18:20; Deut. 10:9) applied only in Palestine and the property was in Cyprus, or perhaps the corrupt religious leaders had become lax in enforcing the law. There is much we do not know about Joseph Barnabas, but this we do know: He was a Spirit-filled man who was an encouragement to the church because he gave his all to the Lord. Not every believer can be like Peter and John, but we can all be like Barnabas and have a ministry of encouragement.

THE HYPOCRISY OF ANANIAS AND SAPPHIRA (5:1–11)

George MacDonald wrote, "Half of the misery in the world comes from trying to *look,* instead of trying to *be,* what one is not." The name that Jesus gave to this practice is "hypocrisy," which simply means "wearing a mask, playing the actor." We must not think that failure to reach our ideals is hypocrisy because no believer lives up to all that he or she knows or has in the Lord. Hypocrisy is *deliberate* deception, trying to make people think we are more spiritual than we really are.

When I was pastoring my first church, the Lord led us to build a new sanctuary. We were not a wealthy congregation, so our plans had to be modest. At one point in the planning, I suggested to the architect that perhaps we could build a simple edifice with a more elaborate facade at the front to make it look more like an expensive church.

"Absolutely not!" he replied. "A church stands for truth and honesty, and any church I design will not have a facade! A building should tell the truth and not pretend to be what it isn't."

Years later, I ran across this poem, which is a sermon in itself:

They build the front just like St. Mark's,
Or like Westminster Abbey;
And then, as if to cheat the Lord,
They make the back parts shabby.

That was the sin of Ananias and Sapphira: putting on a lovely "front" in order to conceal the shabby sin in their lives, sin that cost them their lives.

Ananias means "God is gracious," but he learned that God is also holy, and Sapphira means "beautiful," but her heart was ugly with sin. No doubt some people are shocked when they read that God killed two people just because they lied about a business transaction and about their church giving. But when you consider the features connected with this sin, you have to agree that God did the right thing by judging them.

It is worth noting that the Lord judges sin severely *at the beginning of a new period in salvation history*. Just after the tabernacle was erected, God killed Nadab and Abihu for trying to present "false fire" to the Lord (Lev. 10). He also had Achan killed for disobeying orders after Israel had entered the Promised Land (Josh. 7). While God was certainly not responsible for their sins, He did use these judgments as warnings to the people, and even to us (1 Cor. 10:11–12).

To begin with, the sin of Ananias and Sapphira was *energized by Satan* (Acts 5:3), and that is a serious matter. If Satan cannot defeat the church by attacks from the outside, he will get on the inside and go to work (20:28–31). He knows how to lie to the minds and hearts of church members, even genuine Christians, and get them to follow his orders. We forget that the admonition about the spiritual armor (Eph. 6:10–18) was written to God's people, not to unbelievers, because it is the Christians who are in danger of being used by Satan to accomplish his evil purposes.

Oliver Wendell Holmes wrote, "Sin has many tools, but a lie is the handle which fits them all." Satan is a liar and a murderer (John 8:44). He lied to and *through* this couple, and the lie led to their deaths. When God judged Ananias and Sapphira, He was also judging Satan. He was letting everybody know that He would not tolerate deception in His church.

Their sin was *motivated by pride,* and pride is a sin that God especially hates and judges (Prov. 8:13). No doubt the church was praising God for the generous offering that Barnabas had brought when Satan whispered to the couple, "You can also bask in this kind of glory! You can make others think that you are as spiritual as Barnabas!" Instead of resisting Satan's approaches, they yielded to him and planned their strategy.

Jesus made it very clear that we must be careful how we give, lest the glory that belongs to God should be given to us (Matt. 6:1–4, 19–34). The Pharisees were adept at calling attention to their gifts, and they received the praises of men—but that's all they received! Whatever we possess, God has given to us; we are stewards, not owners. We must use what He gives us for His glory alone (see John 5:44).

Daniel Defoe called pride "the first peer and president of hell." Indeed, it was pride that transformed Lucifer into Satan (Isa. 14:12–15), and it was pride ("Ye shall be as gods") that caused our first parents to sin (Gen. 3). Pride opens the door to every other sin, for once we are more concerned with our reputations than our characters, there is no end to the things we will do just to make ourselves "look good" before others.

A third feature of their sin was especially wicked: Their sin was *directed against God's church.* We have reason to believe that Ananias and Sapphira were believers. The spiritual level of the church at that time was so high that it is doubtful that a mere "professor" could have gotten into the fellowship without being detected. The fact that they were able to lie to the Spirit (Acts 5:3) and tempt the Spirit (v. 9) would indicate that they had the Spirit of God living within.

God loves His church and is jealous over it, for the church was purchased by the blood of God's Son (Acts 20:28; Eph. 5:25) and has been put on earth to glorify Him and do His work. Satan wants to destroy the church, and the easiest way to do it is to use those who are within the fellowship. Had Peter not been discerning, Ananias and Sapphira would have become influential people in the church! Satan would have been working through them to accomplish his purposes!

The church is "the pillar and ground of the truth" (1 Tim. 3:15), and Satan attacks it with his lies. The church is God's temple in which He dwells (1 Cor. 3:16), and Satan wants to move in and dwell there too. The church is God's army (2 Tim. 2:1–4), and Satan seeks to get into the ranks as many traitors as he can. The church is safe so long as Satan is attacking from the outside, but when he gets on the inside, the church is in danger.

It is easy for us to condemn Ananias and Sapphira for their dishonesty, but we need to examine our own lives to see if our profession is backed up by our practice. Do we really mean everything we pray about in public? Do we sing the hymns and gospel songs sincerely or routinely? "These people honor me with their lips, but their hearts are far from me" (Matt. 15:8 NIV). If God killed "religious deceivers" today, how many church members would be left?

What is described in this chapter is not a case of church discipline. Rather it is an example of God's personal judgment. "The Lord shall judge his people. It is a fearful thing to fall into the hands of the living God" (Heb. 10:30–31). Had Ananias and Sapphira judged their own sin, God would not have judged them (1 Cor. 11:31), but they agreed to lie, and God had to deal with them.

Ananias was dead and buried, and Sapphira did not even know it! Satan always keeps his servants in the dark, while God guides His servants in the light (John 15:15). Peter accused her of tempting God's Spirit, that is, deliberately disobeying God and seeing how far God would go (Ex. 17:2; Deut. 6:16). They were actually defying God and daring Him to act—and He acted, with swiftness and finality. "Thou shalt not tempt the Lord thy God" (Matt. 4:7).

We must keep in mind that their sin was not in robbing God of money but in lying to Him and robbing Him of glory. They were not required to sell the property, and having sold it, they were not required to give any of the money to the church (Acts 5:4). Their lust for recognition conceived sin in their hearts (vv. 4, 9), and that sin eventually produced death (James 1:15).

The result was a wave of godly fear that swept over the church and over all those who heard the story (Acts 5:11). We have moved from "great power" and "great grace" (4:33) to "great fear," and all of these ought to be present in the church. "Let us have grace, whereby we may serve God acceptably with reverence and godly fear: For our God is a consuming fire" (Heb. 12:28–29).

THE MINISTRY OF THE APOSTLES (5:12–16)

We have learned that the Spirit-filled church is unified, magnified, and multiplied. Satan wants to divide the church, disgrace the church, and decrease the church, and he will do it, if we let him.

But the church described here completely triumphed over the attacks of Satan! The people were still unified (Acts 5:12), magnified (v. 13), and multiplied (v. 14). Multitudes were added to the Lord, and for the first time, Luke mentions the salvation of women. Both in his gospel and in Acts, Luke has a great deal to say about women and their relationship to Christ and the church. There are at least a dozen references in Acts to women, as Luke shows the key role women played in the apostolic church. This is a remarkable thing when you consider the general position of women in the culture of that day (see Gal. 3:26–28).

God gave the apostles power to perform great miracles. While it is true that some of the ordinary members exercised miraculous powers (Acts 6:8), it was primarily the apostles who did the miracles. These "signs and wonders" were God's way of authenticating their ministry (Rom. 15:18–19; 2 Cor. 12:12; Heb. 2:4).

Just as there were special judgments at the beginning of a new era, so there were also special miracles. We find no miracles performed in Genesis, but at the beginning of the age of law, Moses performed great signs and wonders. Elijah and Elisha were miracle workers at the beginning of the great era of the prophets, and Jesus and the apostles performed signs and wonders when the Gospel Age was inaugurated. Each time God opened a new door, He called man's attention to it. It was His way of saying, "Follow these leaders because I have sent them."

The mighty wonders performed by the apostles were the fulfillment of the Lord's promise that they would do "greater works" in answer to believing prayer (John 14:12–14). When Jesus performed miracles during His ministry on earth, He had three purposes in mind: (1) to show compassion and meet human need; (2) to present His credentials as the Son of God; and (3) to convey spiritual truth. For example, when He fed the five thousand, the miracle met their physical need, revealed Him as the Son of God, and gave Him opportunity to preach a sermon about the Bread of Life (John 6).

The apostolic miracles followed a similar pattern. Peter and John healed the crippled beggar and met his need, but Peter used that miracle to preach a salvation sermon and to prove to the people and the council that he and John were indeed the servants of the living Christ. One of the qualifications for an apostle was that he had seen the risen Christ (Acts 1:22; 1 Cor. 9:1), and since nobody can claim that experience today, there are no apostles in the church. The apostles and prophets laid the foundation for the church (Eph. 2:20), and the pastors, teachers, and evangelists are building on it. If there are no apostles, there can be no "signs of an apostle" as are found in the book of Acts (2 Cor. 12:12).

This certainly does not mean that God is limited and can no longer perform miracles for His people! But it does mean that the need for confirming miracles has passed away. We now have the completed Word of God, and we test teachers by their message, not by miracles (1 John 2:18–29; 4:1–6). And we must keep in mind that Satan is a counterfeiter and well able to deceive the unwary. In the Old Testament, any prophet who performed miracles but, at the same time, led the people away from God's Word, was considered a false prophet and was killed (Deut. 13). The important thing was not the miracles, but whether his message was true to the Word of God.

A radio listener wrote me and wanted to debate this issue with me, insisting that there were instances today of people being raised from the dead. I wrote him a kind letter and asked him to send me the testimonies of the witnesses, the kind of evidence that could be presented in court. He wrote back and honestly admitted that that kind of evidence was not available, but he still believed it because he had heard a TV preacher say it was so. Most of the miracles recorded in the Bible were out in the open for everybody to see, and it would not be difficult to prove them in a court of law.

Peter and the other apostles found themselves ministering as their Lord had ministered, with people coming from all over, bringing their sick and afflicted (Matt. 4:23–25; Mark 1:45; 2:8–12). The Twelve must have found it very difficult to walk down the street, for people crowded around them and laid before them sick people on their pallets. Some of the people even had the superstitious belief that there was healing in Peter's shadow.

It is significant that *all of these people were healed*. There were no failures and nobody was sent away because he or she "did not have faith to be healed." These were days of mighty power when God was speaking to Israel and telling them that Jesus of Nazareth was indeed their Messiah and Savior. "For the Jews require a sign" (1 Cor. 1:22), and God gave signs to them. The important thing was not the healing of the afflicted, but the winning of lost souls, as multitudes were added to the fellowship. The Spirit gave them power for wonders and power for witness (Acts 1:8), for miracles apart from God's Word cannot save the lost.

The greatest miracle of all is the transformation of a lost sinner into a child of God by the grace of God. That is the miracle that meets the greatest need, lasts the longest, and costs the greatest price—the blood of God's Son.

And that is one miracle we can all participate in as we share the message of the gospel, "the power of God unto salvation to every one that believeth" (Rom. 1:16).

QUESTIONS FOR PERSONAL REFLECTION
OR GROUP DISCUSSION

1. How did God give you boldness to witness for Him this past week?

2. Read Acts 4:32–37. How did persecution affect the new church?

3. Read Acts 5:1–11. What principles of giving are found in this section?

4. What do you learn from Barnabas, Ananias, and Sapphira about the proper motivation for giving?

5. Why did Peter confront Ananias and Sapphira publicly?

6. How did Peter know that Ananias was lying about how much money he received for the sale of his property?

7. Why was the hypocrisy of Ananias and Sapphira so dangerous?

8. What does this passage teach us about God?

9. Read Acts 5:12–16. How did the church triumph over Satan's attacks?

10. What can you do to guard against hypocrisy in your life?

Chapter Six

TRUTH AND CONSEQUENCES

(Acts 5:17–42)

A fter Pentecost, the message of the resurrection of Jesus Christ spread rapidly in Jerusalem as Spirit-empowered witnesses shared the gospel with the lost. Signs and wonders accompanied the preaching of the Word, and no one could deny that God was at work in a new way among His ancient people.

But not everybody was happy with the success of the church. The "religious establishment" that had opposed the ministry of Jesus, and then crucified Him, took the same hostile approach toward the apostles. "If they persecuted Me, they will also persecute you," said Jesus. "They will put you out of the synagogues; yes, the time is coming that whoever kills you will think that he offers God service" (John 15:20; 16:2 NKJV). These words were beginning to be fulfilled.

It was the age-old conflict between living truth and dead tradition. The new wine could not be put into the old wineskins, nor could the new cloth be sewn onto the worn-out garments (Matt. 9:14–17). The English martyr Hugh Latimer said, "Whenever you see persecution, there is more than a probability that truth is on the persecuted side."

We see in this account four different responses to God's truth, responses we still see today.

1. The Council: Attacking the Truth (5:17–28)

The high priest and his associates had three reasons for arresting the apostles (this time it was *all* of the apostles) and bringing them to trial. To begin with, Peter and John had not obeyed the official orders to stop preaching in the name of Jesus Christ. They were guilty of defying the law of the nation. Second, the witness of the church was refuting the doctrines held by the Sadducees, giving every evidence that Jesus Christ was alive. Third, the religious leaders were filled with envy ("indignation") at the great success of these untrained and unauthorized men (see Matt. 27:18; Acts 13:45). The traditions of the fathers had not attracted that much attention or gained that many followers in such a short time. It is amazing how much envy can be hidden under the disguise of "defending the faith."

The apostles did not resist arrest or organize a public protest. They quietly went along with the temple guard and actually spent a few hours in the public jail. But during the night, an angel set them free and told them to return to their witnessing in the temple. (The Sadducees, of course, did not believe in angels. See Acts 23:8.) In the book of Acts, you will find several instances of angelic ministries as God cared for His people (Acts 8:26; 10:3, 7; 12:7–11, 23; 27:23). The angels are servants who minister to us as we serve the Lord (Heb. 1:14).

As in Peter's deliverance (Acts 12:7–11), neither the guards nor the leaders knew that the prisoners had been liberated. You are tempted to smile as you imagine the surprised looks on the faces of the guards when they discovered that their most important prisoners were gone. And just imagine the astonishment of the envious members of the Sanhedrin when they heard the report! Here they were trying to *stop* the miracles, but their actions only *multiplied* the miracles!

What a contrast between the apostles and the members of the council. The council was educated, ordained, and approved, and yet they had no ministry of power. The apostles were ordinary laymen, yet God's power was at work in their lives. The council was trying desperately to protect themselves and their dead traditions, while the apostles were risking their lives to share the living Word of God. The dynamic church was enjoying the new; the dead council was defending the old.

You find a variety of emotions in this section: envy (Acts 5:17), bewilderment (v. 24), and fear (v. 26; see 4:21 and Matt. 21:26). Yet, when the apostles came in, the high priest boldly accused them of defying the law and causing trouble. He would not even use the name of Jesus Christ, but instead said "this name" and "this man's blood," lest by speaking His name he would defile his lips or bring down the wrath of God (see John 15:21).

But even this hateful indictment was an admission that the church was increasing and getting the job done! The wrath of man was bringing praise to the Lord (Ps. 76:10). The high priest realized that if the apostles were right, then the Jewish leaders had been wrong in condemning Jesus Christ. Indeed, if the apostles were right, then the council was guilty of His blood (Matt. 27:25; 1 Thess. 2:14–16). As this "trial" progressed, the apostles became the judges and the council became the accused.

2. THE APOSTLES: AFFIRMING THE TRUTH (5:29–32)

The apostles did not change their convictions (Acts 4:19–20). They obeyed God and trusted Him to take care of the consequences. They could not serve two masters, and they had already declared whose side they were on. Had they been diplomats instead of ambassadors (2 Cor. 5:20), they could have pleased everybody and escaped a beating. But they stood firmly for the Lord, and He honored their courage and faith.

Neither did they change their message (Acts 5:30–32). Peter indicted the leaders for the death of Jesus (see Acts 3:13–14; 4:10), and boldly affirmed once again that Jesus Christ had been raised from the dead. Not only was Jesus raised from the dead, but He was also exalted by God to heaven. The work of the Holy Spirit in recent days was evidence that Jesus had returned to heaven and sent His Spirit as He promised. The Sadducees certainly did not rejoice to hear the apostles speak about resurrection from the dead.

That Jesus Christ is at God's right hand is a key theme in the Scriptures. The right hand is, of course, the place of honor, power, and authority. Psalm 110:1 is the basic prophecy, but there are numerous references: Matthew 22:44; Mark 14:62; 16:19; Acts 2:33–34; 5:31; Romans 8:34; Ephesians 1:20; Colossians 3:1; Hebrews 1:3; 8:1; 10:12; 12:2; and 1 Peter 3:22. Soon, Stephen would see Jesus standing at God's right hand (Acts 7:55).

In his second sermon, Peter had called Jesus "the Prince of life" (Acts 3:15); and here he called Him "a Prince and a Savior." The word *Prince* means "a pioneer, one who leads the way, an originator." The Sanhedrin was not interested in pioneering anything; all they wanted to do was protect their vested interests and keep things exactly as they were (see John 11:47–52). As the "Pioneer of life," Jesus saves us and leads us into exciting experiences as we walk "in newness of life" (Rom. 6:4). There are always new trails to blaze.

Hebrews 2:10 calls Him "the [Pioneer] captain of their salvation," for our salvation experience must never become static. The Christian life is not a parking lot; it is a launching pad! It is not enough just to be born again; we must also grow spiritually (2 Peter 3:18) and make progress in our walk. In Hebrews 12:2, Jesus is called "the [Pioneer] author ... of our faith," which suggests that He leads us into new experiences that test our faith and help it to grow. One of the major themes of Hebrews is "let us press on to maturity" (Heb. 6:1 NASB), and we cannot mature unless we follow Christ, the Pioneer, into new areas of faith and ministry.

The title *Savior* was not new to the members of the council, for the word was used for physicians (who save people's lives), philosophers (who solve people's problems), and statesmen (who save people from danger and war). It was even applied to the emperor. But only Jesus Christ is the true and living Savior who rescues from sin, death, and judgment all who will trust Him.

Peter again called the nation to repentance (Acts 2:36; 3:19–26; 4:10–12) and promised that the gift of the Spirit would be given to all who "obey Him." This does not imply that the gift of the Spirit is a reward for obedience, for a gift can be received only by faith. The phrase "obey him" is the same as "obedient to the faith" in Acts 6:7, and means "to obey God's call and trust God's Son." God does not *suggest* that sinners repent and believe; He *commands* it (17:30).

It was a bold witness that the apostles gave before the highest Jewish religious court. The Spirit of God enabled them and they were not afraid. After all, Jesus had promised to be with them and, through His Holy Spirit, empower them for witness and service. They were His witnesses of His resurrection (Acts 1:22; 2:24, 32; 3:15, 26; 4:10), and He would see them through.

3. GAMALIEL: AVOIDING THE TRUTH (5:33–39)

Gamaliel was a Pharisee who probably did not want to see the Sadducees win any victories. He was a scholar highly esteemed by the people, rather liberal in his applications of the law, and apparently moderate in his approach to problems. "When Rabban Gamaliel the Elder died," said the Jews, "the glory of the law ceased and purity and abstinence died." Paul was trained by Gamaliel (Acts 22:3). Gamaliel's "counsel" was unwise and dangerous, but God used it to save the apostles from death. That the Sadducees would heed the words of a Pharisee shows how distinguished a man Gamaliel was.

In spite of the fact that Gamaliel tried to use cool logic rather than overheated emotions, his approach was still wrong. To begin with, he automatically classified Jesus with two rebels, which means *he had already rejected the evidence*. To him, this "Jesus of Nazareth" was just another zealous Jew, trying to set the nation free from Rome. But did Theudas or Judas ever do the things that Jesus did? Were they raised from the dead? With a clever twist of bad logic, Gamaliel convinced the council that there was really nothing to worry about! Troublemakers come and go, so be patient.

Furthermore, Gamaliel assumed that "history repeats itself." Theudas and Judas rebelled, were subdued, and their followers were scattered. Give these Galileans enough time and they too will disband, and you will never again hear about Jesus of Nazareth. While some students do claim to see "cycles" in history, these "cycles" are probably only in the eyes of the beholder. By selecting your evidence carefully, you can prove almost anything from history. The birth, life, death, and resurrection of Jesus Christ had never happened before and would never happen again. God had broken into history and visited this earth!

Gamaliel also had the mistaken idea that if something is not of God, it must fail. But this idea does not take into consideration the sinful nature of man and the presence of Satan in the world. Mark Twain said that a lie runs around the world while truth is still putting on her shoes. In the end, God's truth will be victorious, but meanwhile, Satan can be very strong and influence multitudes of people.

Success is no test of truth, in spite of what the pragmatists say. False cults often grow faster than God's church. This world is a battlefield on which truth and error are in mortal combat, and often it looks as if truth is "on the scaffold," while wrong sits arrogantly on the throne. How long should the council wait to see if the new movement would survive? What tests would they use to determine whether or not it was successful? What is success? No matter how you look at it, Gamaliel's "wisdom" was foolish.

But the biggest weakness of his advice was his motive: He encouraged neutrality when the council was facing a life-and-death issue that demanded decision. "Wait and see!" is actually not neutrality; *it is a definite decision.* Gamaliel was voting "No!" but he was preaching "maybe someday."

There are many matters in life that do not demand a courageous decision of conscience. I had a friend in seminary who became emotionally disturbed because he tried to make every decision a matter of conscience, including the cereal he ate at breakfast and the route he took when he walked to the store. But when we face a serious matter of conscience, we had better examine the evidence carefully. This, Gamaliel refused to do. He lost an opportunity for salvation because he turned the meeting into a petty discussion about Jewish insurrectionists.

Jesus made it clear that it is impossible to be neutral about Him and His message. "He that is not with me is against me; and he that gathereth not with me scattereth abroad" (Matt. 12:30). The members of the council knew the words of Elijah, "How long will you waver between two opinions?" (1 Kings 18:21 NIV). There are times when being neutral means making a quiet (and perhaps cowardly) decision to reject God's offer. It is significant that the first group named among those who go to hell is "the fearful" (Rev. 21:8), the people who knew the truth but were afraid to take their stand.

If Gamaliel was really afraid of fighting against God, why did he not honestly investigate the evidence, diligently search the Scriptures, listen to the witnesses, and ask God for wisdom? This was the opportunity of a lifetime! Daniel Defoe, author of *Robinson Crusoe,* claimed that nobody was born a coward. "Truth makes a man of courage," he wrote, "and guilt makes that man of courage a coward." What some men call caution, God would call cowardice. The apostles were true ambassadors; Gamaliel was really only a "religious politician."

4. The Church: Announcing the Truth (5:40–42)

Part of the council wanted to kill the apostles (Acts 5:33), but Gamaliel's speech tempered their violence. In a compromise move, the council decided to have the apostles beaten, so the men were given thirty-nine strokes (see Deut. 25:1–3; 2 Cor. 11:24). Then the apostles were commanded to stop speaking in the name of Jesus Christ lest something worse happen to them. (Review Acts 2:22; 3:6, 16; 4:10, 12, 17–18, 30.)

When people refuse to deal with disagreements on the basis of principle and truth, they often resort to verbal or physical violence, and sometimes both. The sad thing is that this violence often masquerades as patriotism or as religious zeal. When understanding fails, violence starts to take over, and people begin to destroy each other in the name of their nation or their God. It is tragic that even the history of religion is punctuated with accounts of persecutions and "holy wars." William Temple said that Christians are "called to the hardest of all tasks: to fight without hatred, to resist without bitterness, and in the end, if God grant it so, to triumph without vindictiveness."

How did the apostles respond to this illegal treatment from their nation's religious leaders? They rejoiced! Jesus had told them to expect persecution and had instructed them to rejoice in it (Matt. 5:10–12). The opposition of men meant the approval of God, and it was actually a privilege to suffer for His name (Phil. 1:29).

To paraphrase Phillips Brooks, the purpose of life is to glorify God by the building of character through truth. The Sanhedrin thought that it had won a great victory, when actually the council had experienced a crushing defeat. No doubt they congratulated each other for doing such a good job of defending the faith! But it was the apostles who were the winners because they grew in godliness as they yielded to God's will and suffered for their Master. In later years, Peter would have much to say in his first epistle about the meaning of suffering in the life of the believer, but now he was learning the lessons.

Neither the threats nor the beatings stopped them from witnessing for Jesus Christ. If anything, this persecution only made them trust God more and seek greater power in their ministry. True believers are not "quitters."

The apostles had a commission to fulfill, and they intended to continue as long as their Lord enabled them. Acts 5:42 summarizes the apostolic pattern for evangelism, an excellent pattern for us to follow.

To begin with, they witnessed "daily." This meant that they took advantage of witnessing opportunities no matter where they were (Eph. 5:15–16). *Every* Christian is a witness, either a good one or a bad one, and our witness either draws others to Christ or drives them away. It is a good practice to start each day asking the Lord for the wisdom and grace needed to be a loving witness for Christ that day. If we sincerely look for opportunities and expect God to give them to us, we will never lack for open doors.

D. L. Moody was fearless in his witness for Christ and sought to speak about spiritual matters to at least one soul each day. "How does your soul prosper today?" he would ask; or, "Do you love the Lord? Do you belong to Christ?" Some were offended by his blunt manner, but not a few were led to Christ then and there. "The more we use the means and opportunities we have," he said, "the more will our ability and our opportunities be increased." He also said, "I live for souls and for eternity; I want to win some soul to Christ." He was not satisfied only to address great crowds; he also felt constrained to speak to people personally and urge them to trust Jesus Christ.

The believers witnessed "in the temple." After all, that was where the "religious" people gathered, and it was easier to reach them there. For several years, the church was looked on as another "sect" of the Jewish faith, and both the temple and the many synagogues were open to believers. In his missionary journeys, Paul always went first to the local synagogue or Jewish place of prayer, and he witnessed there until he was thrown out.

My counsel to new Christians has usually been, "Go back to your home and church, be a loving witness for Christ, and stay until they ask you to leave" (see 1 Cor. 7:17–24). The apostles did not abandon the Jewish temple, though they knew the old dispensation was ended and that one day the temple would be destroyed. They were not compromising; they were "buying up the opportunity" to reach more people for Christ.

While I was ministering at the Moody Church in Chicago, it was my joy to lead a pastor to Christ, a gifted man who ministered to a wealthy congregation. He went back to his church and began to share Christ, and numbers of his people were saved. Then the denominational leaders stepped in and started to threaten him with dismissal.

"What do I do?" he asked, and I said, "Stay there until they throw you out. Be loving and kind, but don't give in!" Eventually he was forced out of the church, but not before his witness had influenced many both in the church and in the community. Today, God is using him in a remarkable way to witness for Christ and to train others to witness. He is able to get into churches and groups that might never invite me!

The early Christians also witnessed "in every house." Unlike congregations today, these people had no buildings that were set aside for worship and fellowship. Believers would meet in different homes, worshipping the Lord, listening to teaching, and seeking to win the lost (see Acts 2:46). Paul referred to a number of "house fellowships" when he greeted the saints in Rome (Rom. 16:5, 10–11, 14). The early church took the Word right into the homes, and we should follow their example. This does not mean that it is wrong to have special buildings set aside for church ministry, but only that we must not confine the ministry to the four walls of a church building.

Their ministry went on without ceasing. The authorities had told them to stop witnessing, but they only witnessed all the more! Their motive was not defiance to the law but rather obedience to the Lord. It was not something they turned on and off, depending on the situation. They were "always at it," and they kept at it as long as God gave them opportunities.

The witness of the church included both teaching and preaching, and that is a good balance. The word translated "preach" gives us our English word *evangelize,* and this is the first of fifteen times it is used in Acts. It simply means "to preach the gospel, to share the good news of Jesus Christ." (See 1 Cor. 15:1–8 for the official statement of the gospel message.)

However, proclamation must be balanced with instruction (see Acts 2:42) so that the sinners know *what* to believe and the new converts understand *why* they believed. The message cannot produce fruit unless the person understands it and can make an intelligent decision (Matt. 13:18–23). Believers cannot grow unless they are taught the Word of God (1 Peter 2:1–3).

Finally, it was Jesus Christ who was the center of their witness. That was the very name that the Sanhedrin had condemned! The early church did not go about arguing religion or condemning the establishment: They simply told people about Jesus Christ and urged them to trust in Him. "For we preach not ourselves, but Christ Jesus the Lord" (2 Cor. 4:5). "Ye shall be witnesses unto me" (Acts 1:8).

It was my privilege to speak at a service celebrating the fortieth anniversary of a pastor friend whose ministry has blessed many. A number of his friends shared in the service and quite candidly expressed their love for him and their appreciation for his ministry. My friend became more and more embarrassed as the meeting progressed, and when it came time for me to bring the message, he leaned over and whispered in my ear, "Warren, please tell them about Jesus!"

In his clever and convicting book *The Gospel Blimp,* the late Joe Bayly wrote: "Jesus Christ didn't commit the gospel to an advertising agency; He commissioned disciples."

That commission still stands.

In your life, is it commission—or omission?

QUESTIONS FOR PERSONAL REFLECTION
OR GROUP DISCUSSION

1. Why do people fail to tell the absolute truth all the time?

2. Read Acts 5:17–32. How did the high priest and Sadducees respond to God's truth? Why?

3. What did putting the apostles in jail do to the truth of the gospel?

4. How did Peter and the others affirm the truth of God's Word?

5. What consequences did they suffer for truth or truthfulness?

6. What do you learn about witnessing from Peter's sermons and his response to persecution?

7. Read Acts 5:33–42. What was wrong with Gamaliel's approach to this situation?

8. How did persecution affect the apostles and the church? Why?

9. How will you spread God's truth this week?

Chapter Seven

STEPHEN, THE MAN GOD CROWNED

(Acts 6—7)

There are two words for "crown" in the New Testament: *diadema*, which means "a royal crown" and gives us the English word *diadem*; and *stephanos,* the "victor's crown," which gives us the popular name Stephen. You can inherit a *diadema*, but the only way to get a *stephanos* is to earn it.

Acts 6 and 7 center on the ministry and martyrdom of Stephen, a Spirit-filled believer who was crowned by the Lord. "Be thou faithful unto death, and I will give thee a crown of life" (Rev. 2:10). He was faithful both in life and in death and therefore is a good example for us to follow.

These chapters present Stephen as a faithful believer in four different areas of ministry.

1. STEPHEN THE SERVANT (6:1–7)

The church was experiencing "growing pains," and this was making it difficult for the apostles to minister to everybody. The "Grecians" were the Greek-speaking Jews who had come to Palestine from other nations, and therefore may not have spoken Aramaic, while the "Hebrews" were Jewish residents of the land who spoke both Aramaic and Greek. The fact that the "outsiders" were being neglected created a situation that could have divided the church. However, the apostles handled the problem with great wisdom and did not give Satan any foothold in the fellowship.

When a church faces a serious problem, this presents the leaders and the members with a number of opportunities. For one thing, problems give us the opportunity to examine our ministries and discover what changes must be made. In times of success, it is easy for us to maintain the *status quo,* but this is dangerous. Henry Ward Beecher called success "a last-year's nest from which the birds have flown." Any ministry or organization that thinks its success will go on automatically is heading for failure. We must regularly examine our lives and our ministries lest we start taking things for granted.

The apostles studied the situation and concluded that *they* were to blame: They were so busy serving tables that they were neglecting prayer and the ministry of the Word of God. They had created their own problem because they were trying to do too much. Even today, some pastors are so busy with secondary tasks that they fail to spend adequate time in study and in prayer. This creates a "spiritual deficiency" in the church that makes it easy for problems to develop.

This is not to suggest that serving tables is a menial task, because *every* ministry in the church is important. But it is a matter of priorities; the apostles were doing jobs that others could do just as well. D. L. Moody used to say that it was better to put ten men to work than to try to do the work of ten men. Certainly it is better for you, for the workers you enlist, and for the church as a whole.

Church problems also give us an opportunity to exercise our faith, not only faith in the Lord, but also faith in each other. The leaders suggested a solution, and all the members agreed with it. The assembly selected seven qualified men, and the apostles set them apart for ministry. The church was not afraid to adjust their structure in order to make room for a growing

ministry. When structure and ministry conflict, this gives us an opportunity to trust God for the solution. It is tragic when churches destroy
ministry because they refuse to modify their structure. The apostles were
not afraid to share their authority and ministry with others.

Problems also give us the opportunity to express our love. The Hebrew
leaders and the predominantly Hebrew members selected six men who were
Hellenists and one man who was both a Gentile and a proselyte! What an
illustration of Romans 12:10 and Philippians 2:1–4! When we solve church
problems, we must think of others and not of ourselves only.

We commonly call these seven men of Acts 6 "deacons" because
the Greek noun *diakonos* is used in Acts 6:1 ("ministration"), and the
verb *diakoneo* ("serve") is used in Acts 6:2. However, this title is not
given to them in this chapter, although you find deacons mentioned in
Philippians 1:1 and their qualifications given in 1 Timothy 3:8–13. The
word simply means "a servant." These seven men were humble servants of
the church, men whose work made it possible for the apostles to carry on
their important ministries among the people. Stephen was one of these
men. The emphasis in Stephen's life is on *fullness:* He was full of the
Holy Spirit and wisdom (Acts 6:3, 10), full of faith (v. 5), and full of
power (v. 8). In Scripture, to be "full of" means "to be controlled by."
This man was controlled by the Spirit, faith, wisdom, and power. He was
a God-controlled man yielded to the Holy Spirit, a man who sought to
lead people to Christ.

What was the result? The blessing of God continued and increased! The
church was still unified (Acts 6:5), multiplied (v. 7), and magnified (Acts
v. 8). Acts 6:7 is one of several "summaries" found in the book, statements
that let us know that the story has reached an important juncture (see Acts
2:41; 4:4; 5:12–16; 6:7; 9:31; 12:24; 16:5; 19:20; and 28:31). In Acts 6:7,
Dr. Luke describes the climax of the ministry in Jerusalem, for the persecution following Stephen's death will take the gospel to the Samaritans and

then to the Gentiles. It has been estimated that there were eight thousand Jewish priests attached to the temple ministry in Jerusalem, and "a great company" of them trusted Jesus Christ as Savior!

2. STEPHEN THE WITNESS (6:8–15)

This Spirit-filled man did not limit his ministry to the serving of tables; he also won the lost and even did miracles. Up to this point, it was the apostles who performed the miracles (Acts 2:43; 5:12), but now God gave this power to Stephen also. This was part of His plan to use Stephen to bear witness to the leaders of Israel. Stephen's powerful testimony would be the climax of the church's witness to the Jews. Then the message would go out to the Samaritans and then to the Gentiles.

Jews from many nations resided in Jerusalem in their own "quarters," and some of these ethnic groups had their own synagogues. The freedmen ("libertines") were the descendants of Jews who had previously been in bondage but had won their freedom from Rome. Since Paul came from Tarsus in Cilicia (Acts 21:39), it is possible that he heard Stephen in the synagogue and may have debated with him. However, nobody could match or resist Stephen's wisdom and power (see Luke 21:15). Their only alternative was to destroy him.

Their treatment of Stephen parallels the way the Jewish leaders treated Jesus. First, they hired false witnesses to testify against him. Then, they stirred up the people who accused him of attacking the law of Moses and the temple. Finally, after listening to his witness, they executed him (see Matt. 26:59–62; John 2:19–22).

The Jews were jealous over their law and could not understand how Christ had come to fulfill the law and to bring in the new age. They were proud of their temple and refused to believe that God would permit it to be destroyed. Stephen faced the same spiritual blindness that Jeremiah faced in his ministry (see Jer. 7). The church faced the opposition of Jewish tradition for many years to come, from within its own ranks (Acts 15) and from false teachers coming in from the outside (Gal. 2:4).

The enemy surprised Stephen and arrested him while he was ministering ("having came upon him suddenly" is Wuest's translation of Acts 6:12), and they took him before the same council that had tried Jesus and the apostles. It was not even necessary for Stephen to speak in order to give witness, for the very glow on his face told everybody that he was a servant of God. Certainly the members of the Sanhedrin would recall Moses' shining face (Ex. 34:29–30). It was as though God was saying, "This man is not against Moses! He is like Moses—he is My faithful servant!"

3. STEPHEN THE JUDGE (7:1–53)

This is the longest address in the book of Acts and one of the most important. In it, Stephen reviewed the history of Israel and the contributions made by their revered leaders: Abraham (Acts 7:2–8), Joseph (vv. 9–17), Moses (vv. 18–44), Joshua (v. 45), and David and Solomon (vv. 46–50).

But this address was more than a recitation of familiar facts; it was also a refutation of their indictments against Stephen and a revelation of their own national sins. Stephen proved from their own Scriptures that the Jewish nation was guilty of worse sins than those they had accused him of committing. What were these sins?

They misunderstood their own spiritual roots (vv. 1–8). Stephen's address opens with "the God of glory" and closes with the glory of God (Acts 7:55), and all the time he spoke, his face radiated that same glory! Why? Because Israel was the only nation privileged to have the glory of God as a part of its inheritance (Rom. 9:4). Alas, the glory of God had departed, first from the tabernacle (1 Sam. 4:19–22) and then from the temple (Ezek. 10:4, 18). God's glory had come in His Son (John 1:14), but the nation had rejected Him.

Abraham was the founder of the Hebrew nation, and his relationship to God was one of *grace* and *faith.* God had graciously appeared to him and called him out of heathen darkness into the light of salvation, and Abraham had responded by faith. Abraham was saved by grace, through faith, and not because he was circumcised, kept a law, or worshipped in a temple. All of those things came afterward (see Rom. 4; Gal. 3). He believed the promises of God and it was this faith that saved him.

God promised the land to Abraham's descendants, and then told Abraham that his descendants would suffer in Egypt before they would enter and enjoy the land, and this took place just as God promised. From the very beginning, God had a wise plan for His people, and that plan would be fulfilled as long as they trusted His Word and obeyed His will.

The Jews greatly revered Abraham and prided themselves in being his "children." But they confused physical descent with spiritual experience and depended on their national heritage rather than their personal faith. John the Baptist had warned them about this sin (Matt. 3:7–12) and so had Jesus (John 8:33–59). The Jews were blind to the simple faith of Abraham and the patriarchs, and they had cluttered it with man-made traditions that made salvation a matter of good works, not faith. God has no grand-children. Each of us must be born into the family of God through personal faith in Jesus Christ (John 1:11–13).

The Jews prided themselves in their circumcision, failing to under-stand that the rite was symbolic of an inner spiritual relationship with God (Deut. 10:16; Jer. 4:4; 6:10; Acts 7:51; Gal. 5:1–6; Phil. 3:3; Col. 2:11–12). Over the years, the fulfilling of ritual had taken the place of the enjoyment of reality. This happens in churches even today.

They rejected their God-sent deliverers (vv. 9–36). I have combined the sections dealing with Joseph and Moses because these two Jewish heroes have this in common: They were both rejected as deliverers the first time, but were accepted the second time. Joseph's brethren hated their brother and sold him into servitude, yet later he became their deliverer. They recognized Joseph "at the second time" (Acts 7:13) when they returned to Egypt for more food. Israel rejected Moses when he first tried to deliver them from Egyptian bondage, and he had to flee for his life (Ex. 2:11–22). But when Moses came to them the second time, the nation accepted him and he set them free (Acts 7:35).

These two events illustrate how Israel treated Jesus Christ. Israel rejected their Messiah when He came to them the first time (John 1:11), but when He comes again, they will recognize Him and receive Him (Zech. 12:10; Rev. 1:7). In spite of what they did to His Son, God has not cast away His people (Rom. 11:1–6). Israel today is suffering from a partial spiritual blindness that one day will be taken away (v. 25–32). Individual Jews are being saved, but the nation as a whole is blind to the truth about Jesus Christ.

Before leaving this section, we must deal with some seeming contradictions between Stephen's address and the Old Testament Scriptures.

Genesis 46:26–27 states that seventy people made up the household of Jacob, including Joseph's family already in Egypt, but Stephen claimed that there were seventy-five (Acts 7:14; and see Ex. 1:1–5). The Hebrew text has seventy in both Genesis and Exodus, but the Septuagint (Greek translation of the Old Testament) has seventy-five. Where did the number seventy-five come from in the Septuagint? In their count, the translators included Joseph's grandchildren (1 Chron. 7:14–15, 20–25). Being a Hellenistic Jew, Stephen would naturally use the Septuagint. There is no real contradiction; your total depends on the factors you include.

Acts 7:16 suggests that Jacob was buried at Shechem, but Genesis 50:13 states that he was buried in the cave of Machpelah at Hebron, along with Abraham, Isaac, and Sarah (Gen. 49:30-31,). It was Joseph who was buried at Shechem (Josh. 24:32). It is likely that the children of Israel carried out of Egypt the remains of all the sons of Jacob, and not just Joseph alone, and buried them together in Shechem. The "fathers" mentioned in Acts 7:15 would be the twelve sons of Jacob.

But who purchased the burial place in Shechem—Abraham or Jacob? Stephen seems to say that Abraham bought it, but the Old Testament record says that Jacob did (Gen. 33:18–20). Abraham purchased the cave of Machpelah (Gen. 23:14–20). The simplest explanation is that Abraham actually purchased *both* pieces of property and that Jacob later had to purchase the Shechem property again. Abraham moved around quite a bit, and it would be very easy for the residents of the land to forget or ignore the transactions he had made.

They disobeyed their law (vv. 37–43). Stephen's opponents had accused him of speaking against the sacred law of Moses, but the history of Israel revealed that the nation had repeatedly *broken* that law. God gave the law to His congregation ("church") in the wilderness at Mount Sinai, His living Word through the mediation of angels (see Acts 7:53; Gal. 3:19). No sooner had the people received the law than they disobeyed it by asking Aaron to make them an idol (Ex. 32), and thereby broke the first two of the Ten Commandments (Ex. 20:1–6).

The Jews had worshipped idols in Egypt (Josh. 24:14; Ezek. 20:7–8), and after their settlement in the Promised Land they gradually adopted the gods of the pagan nations around them. God repeatedly disciplined His people and sent them prophets to warn them, until finally He carried them off to Babylon, where they were finally cured of idolatry.

Acts 7:42 should be compared with Romans 1:24–28, for all of these verses describe the judgment of God when He "takes His hands off" and permits sinners to have their own way. When Stephen quoted Amos 5:25–27, he revealed what the Jews had really been doing all those years: In outward form, they were worshipping Jehovah, but in their hearts, they were worshipping foreign gods! The form of the question in Acts 7:42 demands a negative reply: "No, you were not offering those sacrifices to the Lord!"

In this day of "pluralism" of religions and an emphasis on "toleration," we must understand why God hated the pagan religions and instructed Israel to destroy them. To begin with, these religions were unspeakably obscene in their worship of sex and their use of religious prostitutes. Their practices were also brutal, even to the point of offering children as sacrifices to their gods. It was basically demon worship, and it opened the way for all kinds of godless living on the part of the Jews. Had the nation turned from the true God and succumbed to idolatry, it could have meant the end of the godly remnant and the fulfillment of the promise of the Redeemer.

God's law was given to the Jews to protect them from the pagan influence around them, and to enable them to enjoy the blessings of the land. It was the law that made them a holy people, different from the other nations. When Israel broke down that wall of distinction by disobeying God's law, they forfeited the blessing of God and had to be disciplined.

They despised their temple (vv. 44–50). The witnesses accused Stephen of seeking to destroy the temple, but that was exactly what the Jewish nation did! Moses built the tabernacle where God's glory graciously dwelt (Ex. 40:34–38). Solomon built the temple, and once again God's glory came in (1 Kings 8:10–11). But over the years, the worship at the temple degenerated into mere religious formality, and eventually there were idols placed in the temple (2 Kings 21:1–9; Ezek. 8:7–12). Jeremiah warned people against their superstitious faith in the temple and told them that they had turned God's house into a den of thieves (Jer. 7:1–16).

Had the nation heeded their own prophets, they would have escaped the horrors of the Babylonian siege (see the book of Lamentations) and the destruction of their city and temple. Even Solomon recognized the truth that God did not live in buildings (1 Kings 8:27), and the prophet Isaiah made it even clearer (Isa. 66:1–2). We really make nothing for God because everything comes from Him, and how can the Creator of the universe be contained in a man-made building (Acts 17:24)? The Jewish defense of their temple was both illogical and unscriptural.

They stubbornly resisted their God and His truth (vv. 51–53). This is the climax of Stephen's speech, the personal application that cut his hearers to the heart. Throughout the centuries, Israel had refused to submit to God and obey the truths He had revealed to them. Their ears did not hear the truth, their hearts did not receive the truth, and their necks did not bow to the truth. As a result, they killed their own Messiah!

The nation refused to accept the new truth that God was revealing from age to age. Instead of seeing God's truth as seed that produces fruit and more seed, the religious leaders "embalmed" the truth and refused to accept anything new. By the time Jesus came to earth, the truth of God was encrusted with so much tradition that the people could not recognize God's truth when He did present it. Man's dead traditions had replaced God's living truth (see Matt. 15:1–20).

4. STEPHEN THE MARTYR (7:54–60)

You wonder what kind of a world we live in when good and godly men like Stephen can be murdered by religious bigots! But we have similar problems in our "enlightened" age today: taking hostages, bombings that kill or maim innocent people, assassinations, and all in the name of politics or religion. The heart of man has not changed, nor can it be changed apart from the grace of God.

What were the results of Stephen's death? For Stephen, death meant *coronation* (Rev. 2:10). He saw the glory of God and the Son of God standing to receive him to heaven (see Luke 22:69). Our Lord sat down when He ascended to heaven (Ps. 110:1; Mark 16:19), but He stood up to welcome to glory the first Christian martyr (Luke 12:8). This is the last time the title "Son of man" is used in the Bible. It is definitely a messianic title (Dan. 7:13–14), and Stephen's use of it was one more witness that Jesus is indeed Israel's Messiah.

Stephen was not only tried in a manner similar to that of our Lord, but he also died with similar prayers on his lips (Luke 23:34, 46; Acts 7:59–60). A heckler once shouted to a street preacher, "Why didn't God do something for Stephen when they were stoning him?" The preacher replied, "God did do something for Stephen. He gave him the grace to forgive his murderers and to pray for them!" A perfect answer!

For Israel, Stephen's death meant *condemnation*. This was their third murder: They had *permitted* John the Baptist to be killed; they had *asked* for Jesus to be killed; and now they were killing Stephen themselves. When they allowed Herod to kill John, the Jews sinned against God the Father, who had sent John (Matt. 21:28–32). When they asked Pilate to crucify Jesus, they sinned against God the Son (Matt. 21:33–46). When they stoned Stephen, Israel sinned against the Holy Spirit, who was working in and through the apostles (Matt. 10:1–8; Acts 7:51). Jesus said that this sin could never be forgiven (Matt. 12:31–32). Judgment finally came in AD 70 when Titus and the Roman armies destroyed Jerusalem and the temple.

For the church in Jerusalem, the death of Stephen meant *liberation*. They had been witnessing "to the Jew first" ever since Pentecost, but now they would be directed to take the message out of Jerusalem to the Samaritans (Acts 8) and even to the Gentiles (Acts 11:19–26). The opposition of the enemy helped prevent the church from becoming a Jewish "sect" and encouraged them to fulfill the commission of Acts 1:8 and Matthew 28:18–20.

Finally, as far as Saul (Acts 7:58) was concerned, the death of Stephen eventually meant *salvation*. He never forgot the event (22:17–21), and no doubt Stephen's message, prayers, and glorious death were used of the Spirit to prepare Saul for his own meeting with the Lord (Acts 9). God never wastes the blood of His saints. Saul would one day see the same glory that Stephen saw and would behold the Son of God and hear Him speak!

When Christians die, they "fall asleep" (John 11:11; 1 Thess. 4:13). The body sleeps and the spirit goes to be with the Lord in heaven (Acts 7:59; 2 Cor. 5:6–9; Phil. 1:23; Heb. 12:22–23). When Jesus returns, He will bring with Him the spirits of those who have died (1 Thess. 4:14), their bodies will be raised and glorified, and body and spirit will be united in glory to be "forever with the Lord." Even though we Christians weep at the death of a loved one (Acts 8:2), we do not sorrow hopelessly, for we know we shall meet again when we die or when the Lord returns.

God does not call all of us to be martyrs, but He does call us to be "living sacrifices" (Rom. 12:1–2). In some respects, it may be harder to *live* for Christ than to *die* for Him, but if we are living for Him, we will be prepared to die for Him if that is what God calls us to do.

In 1948, Auca martyr Jim Elliot wrote in his journal, "I seek not a long life, but a full one, like You, Lord Jesus." Two years later, he wrote: "I must not think it strange if God takes in youth those whom I would have kept on earth till they were older. God is peopling Eternity, and I must not restrict Him to old men and women."

Like Stephen, Jim Elliot and his four comrades were called on January 8, 1956, to "people Eternity" as they were slain by the people they were seeking to reach. What has happened to the Aucas since then is proof that the blood of the martyrs is indeed the seed of the church. Many Aucas are now Christians.

"Be thou faithful unto death, and I will give thee a crown of life" (Rev. 2:10).

QUESTIONS FOR PERSONAL REFLECTION
OR GROUP DISCUSSION

1. Do you know what your name means? How has your name affected you, if ever?

2. Read Acts 6. What opportunities happened as a result of problems?

3. How did the believers exercise faith in one another?

4. How did they express love to one another?

5. What is important about each qualification for selecting the seven deacons?

6. What are the dangers of putting people who are not spiritually minded in places of leadership?

7. How did Stephen demonstrate stewardship and faithfulness?

8. Read Acts 7. What do you learn about God from Stephen's sermon?

9. What kind of man was Stephen?

10. In what ways would you like to be more like Stephen? How can you follow his example this week?

Chapter Eight

A Church on the Move

(Acts 8)

There is one thing stronger than all the armies in the world," wrote Victor Hugo, "and that is an idea whose time has come."

The gospel of Jesus Christ is much more than an idea. The gospel is "the power of God to salvation for everyone who believes" (Rom. 1:16 NKJV). It is God's "dynamite" for breaking down sin's barriers and setting the prisoners free. Its time had come and the church was on the move. The "salt" was now leaving the "Jerusalem saltshaker" to be spread over all Judea and Samaria, just as the Lord had commanded (Acts 1:8).

The events in Acts 8 center around four different men.

1. A Zealous Persecutor—Saul (8:1–3)

The book of Acts and the Epistles give sufficient data for a sketch of Saul's early life. He was born in Tarsus in Cilicia (Acts 22:3), a "Hebrew of the Hebrews" (see 2 Cor. 11:22; Phil. 3:5), the "son of a Pharisee" (Acts 23:6), and a Roman citizen (16:37; 22:25–28). He was educated in Jerusalem by Gamaliel (22:3) and became a devoted Pharisee (26:4–5; Phil. 3:5). Measured by the law, his life was blameless (Phil. 3:6). He was one of the most promising young Pharisees in Jerusalem, well on his way to becoming a great leader for the Jewish faith (Gal. 1:14).

Saul's zeal for the law was displayed most vividly in his persecution of the church (Gal. 1:13–14; Phil. 3:6). He really thought that persecuting the believers was one way of serving God. He obeyed the light that he had, and when God gave him more light, he obeyed that and became a Christian!

In what ways did Saul persecute the church? He "made havoc of the church," and the verb here describes a wild animal mangling its prey. When Christ spoke to Saul on the Damascus road, He compared him to a beast (Acts 9:5)! The stoning of Stephen, which Saul approved, shows the lengths to which he would go to achieve his purpose. He persecuted both men and women "unto the death" (22:4), entering both houses and synagogues (22:19). He had the believers imprisoned and beaten (22:19; 26:9–11). If they renounced their faith in Jesus Christ ("compelling them to blaspheme"—26:11), they were set free; if they did not recant, they could be killed.

In later years, Paul described himself as "exceedingly mad against them" (Acts 26:11), "a blasphemer [he denounced Jesus Christ], and a persecutor, and injurious [violent]" (1 Tim. 1:13). He was a man with great authority whose devotion to Moses completely controlled his life, and almost destroyed his life. He did it "ignorantly in unbelief" (v. 13), and God showed him mercy and saved him. Saul of Tarsus is the last person in Jerusalem you would have chosen to be the great apostle to the Gentiles!

2. A Faithful Preacher—Philip (8:4–8)

Persecution does to the church what wind does to seed: It scatters it and only produces a greater harvest. The word translated "scattered" (*diaspeiro*, Acts 8:1, 4) means "to scatter seed." The believers in Jerusalem were God's seed, and the persecution was used of God to plant them in new soil so they could bear fruit (Matt. 13:37–38). Some went throughout Judea and Samaria (see Acts 1:8), and others went to more distant fields (Acts 11:19ff.).

The Samaritans were a "half-breed" people, a mixture of Jew and Gentile. The nation originated when the Assyrians captured the ten northern tribes in 732 BC, deported many of the people, and then imported others who intermarried with the Jews. The Samaritans had their own temple and priesthood and openly opposed fraternization with the Jews (John 4:9).

We have no reason to believe that God permitted this persecution because His people were negligent and had to be "forced" to leave Jerusalem. The fact that Saul persecuted believers "even unto strange [foreign] cities" (Acts 26:11) would suggest that their witness was bearing fruit even beyond Jerusalem. Nor should we criticize the apostles for remaining in the city. If anything, we should commend them for their courage and devotion to duty. After all, somebody had to remain there to care for the church.

Because of the witness and death of Stephen, it is possible that the focus of the persecution was against the Hellenistic Jews rather than the "native" Jews. It would be easier for Saul and his helpers to identify the Hellenistic believers, since many of the "native" Jews were still very Jewish and very much attached to the temple. Peter was still keeping a "kosher home" when he was sent to evangelize the household of Cornelius (Acts 10:9–16).

Philip was chosen as a deacon (Acts 6:5), but like Stephen, he grew in his ministry and became an effective evangelist (see 21:8). God directed him to evangelize in Samaria, an area that had been prohibited to the apostles (Matt. 10:5–6). Both John the Baptist and Jesus had ministered there (John 3:23; 4:1ff.), so Philip entered into their labors (John 4:36–38).

The word for preaching in Acts 8:4 means "to preach the gospel, to evangelize"; while the word in Acts 8:5 means "to announce as a herald." Philip was God's commissioned herald to deliver His message to the people of Samaria. To reject the messenger would mean to reject the message and rebel against the authority behind the herald, Almighty God. How people respond to God's messenger and God's message is serious business.

Philip not only declared God's Word, but he also demonstrated God's power by performing miracles. It was the apostles who had majored on miracles (Acts 2:43; 5:12), yet both Stephen and Philip did signs and wonders by the power of God (6:8). However, the emphasis here is on the Word of God: The people gave heed to the Word because they saw the miracles, and by believing the Word, they were saved. Nobody was ever saved simply because of miracles (John 2:23–25; 12:37–41).

Great persecution (Acts 8:1) plus the preaching of the gospel resulted in great joy! Both in his gospel and in the book of Acts, Luke emphasizes the joy of salvation (Luke 2:10; 15:7, 10; 24:52; Acts 8:8; 13:52; 15:3). The people of Samaria who heard the gospel and believed were delivered from physical affliction, demonic control, and, most important, from their sins. No wonder there was great joy!

The gospel had now moved from "Jewish territory" into Samaria where the people were part Jew and part Gentile. God in His grace had built a bridge between two estranged peoples and made the believers one in Christ, and soon He would extend that bridge to the Gentiles and include them as well. Even today, we need "bridge builders" like Philip, men and women who will carry the gospel into pioneer territory and dare to challenge ancient prejudices. "Into all the world … the gospel to every creature" is still God's commission to us.

3. A CLEVER DECEIVER—SIMON THE SORCERER (8:9–25)

It is a basic principle in Scripture that wherever God sows His true believers, Satan will eventually sow his counterfeits (Matt. 13:24–30, 36–43).

This was true of the ministry of John the Baptist (3:7ff.) and Jesus (23:15, 33; John 8:44), and it would be true of Paul's ministry also (Acts 13:6ff.; 2 Cor. 11:1–4, 13–15). The enemy comes as a lion to devour, and when that approach fails, he comes as a serpent to deceive. Satan's tool in this case was a sorcerer named Simon.

The word translated "bewitched" in Acts 8:9 and 11 simply means "astounded, confounded." It is translated "wondered" in Acts 8:13. The people were amazed at the things that Simon did, and therefore, they believed the things that he said. They considered him "the great power of God." Simon's sorcery was energized by Satan (2 Thess. 2:1–12) and was used to magnify himself, while Philip's miracles were empowered by God and were used to glorify Christ. Simon started to lose his following as the Samaritans listened to Philip's messages, believed on Jesus Christ, were born again, and were baptized.

What does it mean that "Simon himself believed" (Acts 8:13)? We can answer that question best by asking another one: What was the basis of his "faith"? His faith was not in the Word of God, but in the miracles he saw Philip perform, and there is no indication that Simon repented of his sins. He certainly did not believe with *all* his heart (Acts 8:37). His faith was like that of the people of Jerusalem who witnessed our Lord's miracles (John 2:23–25), or even like that of the demons (James 2:19). Simon continued with Philip, not to hear the Word and learn more about Jesus Christ, but to witness the miracles and perhaps learn how they were done.

It is important to note that the Samaritans did not receive the gift of the Holy Spirit when they believed. It was necessary for two of the apostles, Peter and John, to come from Jerusalem, put their hands on the converts, and impart to them the gift of the Spirit. Why? Because God wanted to unite the Samaritan believers with the original Jewish church in Jerusalem. He did not want two churches that would perpetuate the division and conflict that had existed for centuries. Jesus had given Peter the "keys of the kingdom of heaven" (Matt. 16:13–20), which meant that Peter had the privilege of "opening the door of faith" to others. He opened the door to the Jews at Pentecost, and now he opened the door to the Samaritans. Later, he would open the door of faith to the Gentiles (Acts 10).

Remember too that the first ten chapters of Acts record a period of transition, from the Jew to the Samaritan to the Gentile. God's pattern for today is given in Acts 10: The sinner hears the gospel, believes, receives the gift of the Spirit, and then is baptized. It is dangerous to base any doctrine or practice *only* on what is recorded in Acts 1—10, for you might be building on that which was temporary and transitional. Those who claim we must be baptized to receive the gift of the Spirit (Acts 2:38) have a hard time explaining what happened to the Samaritans, and those who claim we must have "the laying on of hands" to receive the Spirit have a difficult time with Acts 10. Once you accept Acts 1—10 as a transitional period in God's plan, with Acts 10 being the climax, the problems are solved.

The wickedness of Simon's heart was fully revealed by the ministry of the two apostles. Simon not only wanted to perform miracles, but he also wanted the power to convey the gift of the Holy Spirit to others—and he was quite willing to pay for this power! It is this passage that gives us the word *simony,* which means "the buying and selling of church offices or privileges."

As you study the book of Acts, you will often find the gospel in conflict with money and "big business." Ananias and Sapphira lost their lives because they lied about their gift (Acts 5:1–11). Paul put a fortune-teller out of business in Philippi and ended up in jail (16:16–24). He also gave the silversmiths trouble in Ephesus and helped cause a riot (19:23–41). The early church had its priorities straight: It was more important to preach the Word than to win the support of the wealthy and influential people of the world.

Peter's words to Simon give every indication that the sorcerer was not a converted man. "Thy money perish with thee!" is pretty strong language to use with a believer. He had neither "part or lot in this matter" ("this word"), and his heart was not right before God. While it is not out of place for believers to repent (see Rev. 2—3), the command to repent is usually given to unbelievers. The word *thought* in Acts 8:22 means "plot or scheme" and is used in a bad sense. The fact that Simon was "in the gall of bitterness" and "the bond of iniquity" would indicate that he had never truly been born again (Acts 8:23; cf. Deut. 29:18; Heb. 12:15).

Simon's response to these severe words of warning was not at all encouraging. He was more concerned about avoiding judgment than getting right with God! There is no evidence that he repented and sought forgiveness. A sinner who wants the prayers of others but who will not pray himself is not going to enter God's kingdom.

This episode only shows how close a person can come to salvation and still not be converted. Simon heard the gospel, saw the miracles, gave a profession of faith in Christ, and was baptized, and yet he was never born again. He was one of Satan's clever counterfeits, and had Peter not exposed the wickedness of his heart, Simon would have been accepted as a member of the Samaritan congregation!

Even though the persecution was still going on, Peter and John returned to Jerusalem, preaching the gospel in "many villages of the Samaritans" as they went their way. They lost no opportunity to share the good news with others now that the doors were open in Samaria.

4. A Concerned Seeker—an Ethiopian (8:26–40)

Philip was not only a faithful preacher, he was also an obedient personal worker. Like his Master, he was willing to leave the crowds and deal with one lost soul. The angel could have told this Ethiopian official how to be saved, but God has not given the commission to angels: He has given it to His people. Angels have never personally experienced God's grace; therefore, they can never bear witness of what it means to be saved.

D. L. Moody once asked a man about his soul, and the man replied, "It's none of your business!" "Oh, yes, it is my business!" Moody said, and the man immediately exclaimed, "Then you must be D. L. Moody!" It is every Christian's business to share the gospel with others, and to do it without fear or apology.

Philip's experience ought to encourage us in our own personal witness for the Lord. To begin with, God directed Philip to the right person at the right time. You and I are not likely to have angels instruct us, but we can know the guidance of the Holy Spirit in our witnessing if we are walking in the Spirit and praying for God's direction.

Late one afternoon, I was completing my pastoral calling and I felt impressed to make one more visit to see a woman who was faithfully attending church but was not a professed Christian. At first, I told myself that it was foolish to visit her that late in the day, since she was probably preparing a meal for her family. But I went anyway and discovered that she had been burdened about her sins all that day! Within minutes, she opened her heart to Christ and was born again. Believe me, I was glad I obeyed the leading of the Spirit!

This court official did not come from what we know today as Ethiopia; his home was in ancient Nubia, located south of Egypt. Since he was a eunuch, he could not become a full Jewish proselyte (Deut. 23:1), but he was permitted to become a "God fearer" or "a proselyte of the gate." He was concerned enough about his spiritual life to travel over two hundred miles to Jerusalem to worship God, but his heart was still not satisfied.

This Ethiopian represents many people today who are religious, read the Scriptures, and seek the truth, yet do not have saving faith in Jesus Christ. They are sincere, but they are lost! They need someone to show them the way.

As Philip drew near to the chariot, he heard the man reading from the prophet Isaiah. (It was customary in those days for students to read out loud.) God had already prepared the man's heart to receive Philip's witness! If we obey the Lord's leading, we can be sure that God will go before us and open the way for our witness.

Isaiah 53 was the passage he was reading, the prophecy of God's Suffering Servant. Isaiah 53 describes our Lord Jesus Christ in His birth (vv. 1–2), life and ministry (v. 3), substitutionary death (vv. 4–9), and victorious resurrection (vv. 10–12). Isaiah 53:4 should be connected with 1 Peter 2:24; Isaiah 53:7 with Matthew 26:62–63; Isaiah 53:9 with Matthew 27:57–60; and Isaiah 53:12 with Luke 23:34, 37.

The Ethiopian focused on Isaiah 53:7–8, which describes our Lord as the willing Sacrifice for sinners, even to the point of losing His human rights. As Philip explained the verses to him, the Ethiopian began to understand the gospel because the Spirit of God was opening his mind to God's truth. It is not enough for the lost sinner to desire salvation; he must also understand God's plan of salvation. It is the heart that understands the Word that eventually bears fruit (Matt. 13:23).

The idea of substitutionary sacrifice is one that is found from the beginning of the Bible to the end. God killed animals so that He might clothe Adam and Eve (Gen. 3:21). He provided a ram to die in the place of Isaac (Gen. 22:13). At Passover, innocent lambs died for the people of Israel (Ex. 12), and the entire Jewish religious system was based on the shedding of blood (Lev. 17, especially v. 11). Jesus Christ is the fulfillment of both the Old Testament types and the prophecies (John 1:29; Rev. 5).

"Faith cometh by hearing, and hearing by the word of God" (Rom. 10:17). The Ethiopian believed on Jesus Christ and was born again! So real was his experience that he insisted on stopping the caravan and being baptized immediately! He was no "closet Christian"; he wanted everybody to know what the Lord had done for him.

How did he know that believers were supposed to be baptized? Perhaps Philip had included this in his witness to him, or perhaps he had even seen people baptized while he was in Jerusalem. We know that Gentiles were baptized when they became Jewish proselytes. Throughout the book of Acts, baptism is an important part of the believer's commitment to Christ and witness for Christ.

While Acts 8:37 is not found in all the New Testament manuscripts, there is certainly nothing in it that is unbiblical (Rom. 10:9–10). In the days of the early church, converts were not baptized unless they first gave a clear testimony of their faith in Jesus Christ. And keep in mind that the Ethiopian was speaking not only to Philip but also to those in the caravan who were near his chariot. He was an important man, and you can be sure that his attendants were paying close attention.

Philip was caught away to minister elsewhere (compare 1 Kings 18:12), but the treasurer "went on his way rejoicing" (see Acts 8:39). God did not permit Philip to do the necessary discipling of this new believer, but surely He provided for it when the man arrived home. Even though he was a eunuch, the Ethiopian was accepted by God (see Isa. 56:3–5)!

Philip ended up at Azotus, about twenty miles from Gaza, and then made his way to Caesarea, a journey of about sixty miles. Like Peter and John, Philip preached his way home (Acts 8:25) as he told others about the Savior. Twenty years later, we find Philip living in Caesarea and still serving God as an evangelist (Acts 21:8ff.).

As you trace the expansion of the gospel during this transition period (Acts 2—10), you see how the Holy Spirit reaches out to the whole world. In Acts 8, the Ethiopian who was converted was a descendant of Ham (Gen. 10:6, where "Cush" refers to Ethiopia). In Acts 9, Saul of Tarsus will be saved, a Jew and therefore a descendant of Shem (Gen. 10:21ff.). In Acts 10, the Gentiles find Christ, and they are the descendants of Japheth (Gen. 10:2–5). The whole world was peopled by Shem, Ham, and Japheth (v. 1), and God wants the whole world—all of their descendants—to hear the message of the gospel (Matt. 28:18–20; Mark 16:15).

In October 1857, J. Hudson Taylor began to minister in Ningpo, China, and he led a Mr. Nyi to Christ. The man was overjoyed and wanted to share his faith with others.

"How long have you had the good tidings in England?" Mr. Nyi asked Hudson Taylor one day. Taylor acknowledged that England had known the gospel for many centuries.

"My father died seeking the truth," said Mr. Nyi. "Why didn't you come sooner?"

Taylor had no answer to that penetrating question.

How long have *you* known the gospel?

How far have you shared it personally?

QUESTIONS FOR PERSONAL REFLECTION
OR GROUP DISCUSSION

1. How was the gospel sown in your life before you became a believer?

2. In what ways is spreading the gospel like sowing seeds?

3. Read Acts 8:1–3. What kind of man was Saul?

4. Read Acts 8:4–40. How did God use Philip? Why do you suppose He worked this way in this case?

5. What do you learn about faith from Simon's words and actions?

6. By contrast, what sort of faith do we want to foster in others when we demonstrate and explain the gospel?

7. How can you incorporate Philip's example into your own witnessing?

8. What is the importance of baptism in the Christian's life?

9. How did God use circumstances in this chapter to spread the gospel?

10. How did God use the normal routine of life to spread the gospel?

11. How can you witness more in your daily routine this week?

Chapter Nine

GOD ARRESTS SAUL

(Acts 9:1–31)

The conversion of Saul of Tarsus, the leading persecutor of the Christians, was perhaps the greatest event in church history after the coming of the Spirit at Pentecost. The next great event would be the conversion of the Gentiles (Acts 10), and Saul (Paul) would become the apostle to the Gentiles. God was continuing to work out His plan to bring the gospel to the whole world.

"Paul was a great man," said Charles Spurgeon, "and I have no doubt that on the way to Damascus he rode a very high horse. But a few seconds sufficed to alter the man. How soon God brought him down!"

The account of the conversion of Saul of Tarsus is given three times in Acts, in chapters 9, 22, and 26. According to the record before us, Saul experienced four meetings that together transformed his life.

1. HE MET JESUS CHRIST (9:1–9)

When you look at Saul *on the road* (Acts 9:1–2), you see a very zealous man who actually thought he was doing God a service by persecuting the church. Had you stopped him and asked for his reasons, he might have said something like this:

"Jesus of Nazareth is dead. Do you expect me to believe that a crucified nobody is the promised Messiah? According to our law, anybody who is hung on a tree is cursed [Deut. 21:23]. Would God take a cursed false prophet and make him the Messiah? No! His followers are preaching that Jesus is both alive and doing miracles through them. But their power comes from Satan, not God. This is a dangerous sect, and I intend to eliminate it before it destroys our historic Jewish faith!"

In spite of his great learning (Acts 26:24), Saul was spiritually blind (2 Cor. 3:12–18) and did not understand what the Old Testament really taught about the Messiah. Like many others of his countrymen, he stumbled over the cross (1 Cor. 1:23) because he depended on his own righteousness and not on the righteousness of God (Rom. 9:30—10:13; Phil. 3:1–10). Many self-righteous religious people today do not see their need for a Savior and resent it if you tell them they are sinners.

Saul's attitude was that of an angry animal whose very breath was dangerous (see Acts 8:3)! Like many other rabbis, he believed that the law had to be obeyed before Messiah could come, and yet these "heretics" were preaching against the law, the temple, and the traditions of the fathers (6:11–13). Saul wasted the churches in Judea (Gal. 1:23) and then got authority from the high priest to go as far as Damascus to hunt down the disciples of Jesus. This was no insignificant enterprise, for the authority of the highest Jewish council was behind him (Acts 22:5).

Damascus had a large Jewish population, and it has been estimated that there could well have been thirty to forty synagogues in the city. The fact that there were already believers there indicates how effective the church had been in getting out the message. Some of the believers may have fled the persecution in Jerusalem, which explains why Saul wanted authority to bring them back. Believers were still identified with the Jewish synagogues, for the break with Judaism would not come for a few years. (See James 2:2, where "assembly" is "synagogue" in the original Greek.)

Saul suddenly found himself *on the ground* (Acts 9:4)! It was not a heat stroke or an epileptic seizure that put him there, but a personal meeting with Jesus Christ. At midday (Acts 22:6), he saw a bright light from heaven and heard a voice speaking his name (vv. 6–11). The men with him also fell to the earth (26:14) and heard the sound, but they could not understand the words spoken from heaven. They stood to their feet in bewilderment (9:7), hearing Saul address someone, but not knowing what was happening.

Saul of Tarsus made some wonderful discoveries that day. To begin with, he discovered to his surprise that Jesus of Nazareth was actually *alive!* Of course, the believers had been constantly affirming this (Acts 2:32; 3:15; 5:30–32), but Saul had refused to accept their testimony. If Jesus was alive, then Saul had to change his mind about Jesus and His message. He had to repent, a difficult thing for a self-righteous Pharisee to do.

Saul also discovered that he was a lost sinner who was in danger of the judgment of God. "I am Jesus, whom you are persecuting" (Acts 9:5 NKJV). Saul thought he had been serving God, when in reality he had been persecuting the Messiah! When measured by the holiness of Jesus Christ, Saul's good works and legalistic self-righteousness looked like filthy rags (Isa. 64:6; Phil. 3:6–8). All of his values changed. He was a new person because he trusted Jesus Christ.

The Lord had a special work for Saul to do (Acts 26:16–18). The Hebrew of the Hebrews would become the apostle to the Gentiles; the persecutor would become a preacher; and the legalistic Pharisee would become the great proclaimer of the grace of God. Up to now, Saul had been like a wild animal, fighting against the goads, but now he would become a vessel of honor, the Lord's "tool," to preach the gospel in the regions beyond. What a transformation!

Some thirty years later, Paul wrote that Christ had "apprehended him" on the Damascus road (Phil. 3:12). Saul was out to arrest others when the Lord arrested him. He had to lose his religion before he could gain the righteousness of Christ. His conversion experience is unique, because sinners today certainly do not hear God's voice or see blinding heavenly

134 \ Be Dynamic

lights. However, Paul's experience is an example of how Israel will be saved when Jesus Christ returns and reveals Himself to them (Zech. 12:10; Matt. 24:29ff.; 1 Tim. 1:12–16). His salvation is certainly a great encouragement to any lost sinner, for if "the chief of sinners" could be saved, surely anybody can be saved!

It is worth noting that the men who were with Saul saw the light, but did not see the Lord, and they heard the sound, but did not hear the voice speaking the words (see John 12:27–29). We wonder if any of them later trusted in Christ because of Saul's testimony. He definitely saw the glorified Lord Jesus Christ (1 Cor. 15:7–10).

The men led Saul *into the city* (Acts 9:8–9), for the angry bull (v. 1) had now become a docile lamb! The leader had to be led because the vision had left him blind. His spiritual eyes had been opened, but his physical eyes were closed. God was thoroughly humbling Saul and preparing him for the ministry of Ananias. He fasted and prayed (v. 9) for three days, during which time he no doubt started to "sort out" what he believed. He had been saved by grace, not by law, through faith in the living Christ. God began to instruct Saul and show him the relationship between the gospel of the grace of God and the traditional Mosaic religion that he had practiced all his life.

2. HE MET ANANIAS (9:10–19)

Ananias was a devout Jew (Acts 22:12) who was a believer in Jesus Christ. He knew what kind of reputation Saul had and that he was coming to Damascus to arrest believers. It was up to a week's journey from Jerusalem to Damascus, but some of the Jerusalem Christians had gotten to the city first in order to warn the saints.

It is interesting to note in Acts 9 the different names used for God's people: disciples (Acts 9:1, 10, 19, 25–26, 36, 38), those of the way (v. 2), saints (vv. 13, 32, 41), all that call on God's name (vv. 14, 21), and brethren (vv. 17, 30). We use the word *Christian* most frequently, and yet that name did not appear on the scene until later (11:26). "Disciples" is the name that is used most in the book of Acts, but you do not find it used in the Epistles. There the name "saints" is the most frequently used title for God's people.

Ananias was available to do God's will, but he certainly was not anxious to obey! The fact that Saul was "praying" instead of "preying" should have encouraged Ananias. "Prayer is the autograph of the Holy Ghost upon the renewed heart," said Charles Spurgeon (Rom. 8:9, 14–16). Instead of trusting himself, Saul was now trusting the Lord and waiting for Him to show him what to do. In fact, Saul had already seen a vision of a man named Ananias (Hananiah = "the Lord is gracious") coming to minister to him; so, how could Ananias refuse to obey?

Acts 9:15 is a good summary of Paul's life and ministry. It was all of grace, for he did not choose God; it was God who chose him (2 Thess. 2:13). He was God's vessel (2 Tim. 2:20–21), and God would work in and through him to accomplish His purposes (Eph. 2:10; Phil. 2:12–13). God's name would be glorified as His servant would take the gospel to Jews and Gentiles, kings and commoners, and as he would suffer for Christ's sake. This is the first reference in the book of Acts to the gospel going to the Gentiles (see also Acts 22:21; 26:17).

Once convinced, Ananias lost no time going to the house of Judas and ministering to the waiting Saul. The fact that he called him "brother" must have brought joy to the heart of the blinded Pharisee. Saul not only heard Ananias's voice, but he felt his hands (Acts 9:12, 17). By the power of God, his eyes were opened and he could see! He was also filled with the Holy Spirit and baptized, and then he ate some food.

The King James Version of Acts 22:16 conveys the impression that it was necessary for Saul to be baptized in order to be saved, but that was not the case. Saul washed away his sins by "calling on the Lord" (Acts 2:21; Rom.

10:13). Kenneth Wuest translates Acts 22:16, "Having arisen, be baptized and wash away your sins, having previously called upon His name." In the Greek, it is not a present participle ("calling"), but an aorist participle ("having called"). His calling on the Lord preceded his baptism.

Saul tarried with the believers in Damascus and no doubt learned from them. Imagine what it would be like to disciple the great apostle Paul! He discovered that they were loving people, undeserving of the persecution he had inflicted on them, and that they knew the truth of God's Word and only wanted to share it with others.

Before we leave this section, we should emphasize some practical lessons that all believers ought to learn.

To begin with, *God can use even the most obscure saint.* Were it not for the conversion of Saul, we would never have heard of Ananias, and yet Ananias had an important part to play in the ongoing work of the church. Behind many well-known servants of God are lesser-known believers who have influenced them. God keeps the books and will see to it that each servant will get a just reward. The important thing is not fame but faithfulness (1 Cor. 4:1–5).

The experience of Ananias also reminds us that we *should never be afraid to obey God's will.* Ananias at first argued with the Lord and gave some good reasons why he should not visit Saul. But the Lord had everything under control, and Ananias obeyed by faith. When God commands, we must remember that He is working "at both ends of the line," and that His perfect will is always the best.

There is a third encouragement: *God's works are always balanced.* God balanced a great public miracle with a quiet meeting in the house of Judas. The bright light and the voice from heaven were dramatic events, but the visit of Ananias was somewhat ordinary. The hand of God pushed Saul from his "high horse," but God used the hand of a man to bring Saul what he most needed. God spoke from heaven, but He also spoke through an obedient disciple who gave the message to Saul. The "ordinary" events were just as much a part of the miracle as were the extraordinary.

Finally, *we must never underestimate the value of one person brought to Christ.* Peter was ministering to thousands in Jerusalem, and Philip had seen a great harvest among the Samaritan people, but Ananias was sent to only one man. Yet what a man! Saul of Tarsus became Paul the apostle, and his life and ministry have influenced people and nations ever since. Even secular historians confess that Paul is one of the significant figures in world history.

On April 21, 1855, Edward Kimball led one of the young men in his Sunday school to faith in Christ. Little did he realize that Dwight L. Moody would one day become the world's leading evangelist. The ministry of Norman B. Harrison in an obscure Bible conference was used of God to bring Theodore Epp to faith in Christ, and God used Theodore Epp to build the Back to the Bible ministry around the world. Our task is to lead men and women to Christ; God's task is to use them for His glory; and every person is important to God.

3. HE MET THE OPPOSITION (9:20–25)

Saul immediately began to proclaim the Christ that he had persecuted, declaring boldly that Jesus is the Son of God. This is the only place in Acts that you find this title, but Paul used it in his epistles at least fifteen times. It was a major emphasis in his ministry. The dramatic change in Saul's life was a source of wonder to the Jews at Damascus. Every new convert's witness for Christ ought to begin right where he is, so Saul began his ministry first in Damascus (Acts 26:20).

It is likely that Saul's visit to Arabia (Gal. 1:17) took place about this time. Had Dr. Luke included it in his account, he would have placed it between Acts 9:21 and 22. We do not know how long he remained in Arabia, but we do know that after three years, Saul was back in Jerusalem (v. 18).

Why did he go to Arabia? Probably because the Lord instructed him to get alone so that He might teach Saul His Word. There were many things that would have to be clarified in Saul's mind before he could minister effectively as an apostle of Jesus Christ. If Saul went to the area near Mount Sinai (Gal. 4:25), it took considerable courage and strength for such a journey. Perhaps it was then that he experienced "perils of robbers" and "perils in the wilderness" (2 Cor. 11:26). It is also possible that he did some evangelizing while in Arabia, because when he returned to Damascus, he was already a marked man.

The important thing about this Arabian sojourn is the fact that Saul did not "confer with flesh and blood" but received his message and mandate directly from the Lord (see Gal. 1:10–24). He did not borrow anything from the apostles in Jerusalem, because he did not even meet them until three years after his conversion.

When Saul returned to Damascus, he began his witness afresh, and the Jews sought to silence him. Now he would discover what it meant to be the hunted instead of the hunter! This was but the beginning of the "great things" he would suffer for the name of Christ (Acts 9:16). How humiliating it must have been for Saul to be led into Damascus as a blind man and then smuggled out like a common criminal (see 2 Cor. 11:32–33).

Throughout his life, the great apostle was hated, hunted, and plotted against by both Jews and Gentiles ("in perils of my own countrymen, in perils of the Gentiles"—2 Cor. 11:26 NKJV). As you read the book of Acts, you see how the opposition and persecution increase, until the apostle ends up a prisoner in Rome (Acts 13:45, 50; 14:19; 17:5, 13; 18:12; 20:3, 19; 21:10–11, 27ff.). But he counted it a privilege to suffer for the sake of Christ, and so should we. "Yea, and all that will live godly in Christ Jesus shall suffer persecution" (2 Tim. 3:12).

4. He Met the Jerusalem Believers (9:26–31)

There were two stages in Saul's experience with the church in Jerusalem.

(1) Saul rejected (v. 26). At first, the believers in the Jerusalem church were afraid of him. Saul "kept trying" (literal Greek) to get into their fellowship, but they would not accept him. For one thing, they were afraid of him and probably thought that his new attitude of friendliness was only a trick to get into their fellowship so he could have them arrested. They did not believe that he was even a disciple of Jesus Christ, let alone an apostle who had seen the risen Savior.

Their attitude seems strange to us, for surely the Damascus saints had gotten word to the church in Jerusalem that Saul had been converted and was now preaching the Word. Perhaps Saul's "disappearance" for almost three years gave an air of suspicion to his testimony. Where had he been? What was he doing? Why had he waited so long to contact the Jerusalem elders? Furthermore, what right did he have to call himself an apostle when he had not been selected by Jesus Christ? There were many unanswered questions that helped create an atmosphere of suspicion and fear.

(2) Saul accepted (vv. 27–31). It was Barnabas who helped the Jerusalem church accept Saul. We met Joseph, the "son of encouragement," in Acts 4:36–37, and we will meet him again as we continue to study Acts. Barnabas "took hold" of Saul, brought him to the church leaders, and convinced them that Saul was both a believer and a chosen apostle. He had indeed seen the risen Christ (1 Cor. 9:1). It is not necessary to invent some "hidden reason" why Barnabas befriended Saul. This was just the nature of the man: He was an encouragement to others.

There seems to be a contradiction between Acts 9:27 and Galatians 1:18–19. How could Barnabas introduce Saul to "the apostles" (plural) if Peter was the only apostle Saul met? Dr. Luke is obviously using the word "apostle" in the wider sense of "spiritual leader." Even Galatians 1:19 calls James, the brother of the Lord, an apostle, and Barnabas is called an apostle in Acts 14:4 and 14. In his epistles, Paul sometimes used "apostle" to designate a special messenger or agent of the church (Rom. 16:7; 2 Cor. 8:23; Phil. 2:25, original Greek). So, there really is no contradiction; it is the leaders of the Jerusalem church that Saul met.

Saul began to witness to the Greek-speaking Jews, the Hellenists that had engineered the trial and death of Stephen (Acts 6:9–15). Saul was one of them, having been born and raised in Tarsus, and no doubt he felt an obligation to take up the mantle left by Stephen (Acts 22:20). The Hellenistic Jews were not about to permit this kind of witness, so they plotted to kill him.

At this point, we must read Acts 22:17–21. God spoke to Saul in the temple and reminded him of his commission to take the message to the Gentiles (Acts 9:15). Note the urgency of God's command: "Quick! … Leave Jerusalem immediately, because they will not accept your testimony about me" (22:18 NIV). Saul shared this message with the church leaders, and they assisted him in returning to his native city, Tarsus. The fact that they believed Saul's testimony about the vision is proof that he had been fully accepted by the church.

We will not meet Saul again until Acts 11:25, when once more it is Barnabas who finds him and brings him to the church at Antioch where they ministered together. That took place about seven years after Saul left Jerusalem, about ten years after his conversion. We have every reason to believe that Saul used Tarsus as his headquarters for taking the gospel to the Gentiles in that part of the Roman Empire. He ministered "in the regions of Syria and Cilicia" (Gal. 1:21) and established churches there (Acts 15:41). Some Bible scholars believe that the Galatian churches were founded at this time.

It is likely that some of the trials listed in 2 Corinthians 11:24–26 occurred during this period. Only one Roman beating is recorded in Acts (16:22), which leaves two not accounted for. Likewise, the five Jewish beatings are not recorded either in Acts or the Epistles. Luke tells us about only one shipwreck (Acts 27), but we have no record of the other two. Anyone who thinks that the apostle was taking a vacation during those years is certainly in error!

Acts 9:31 is another of Luke's summaries that he regularly dropped into the book (Acts 2:46–47; 4:4, 32; 5:12–14). Note that the geographic locations parallel those given in Acts 1:8. Luke is telling us that the message was going out just as the Lord had commanded. Soon, the center would be Antioch, not Jerusalem, and the key leader Paul, not Peter, and the gospel would be taken to the uttermost part of the earth.

It was a time of "peace" for the churches, but not a time of complacency, for they grew both spiritually and numerically. They seized the opportunity to repair and strengthen their sails before the next storm began to blow! The door of faith had been opened to the Jews (Acts 2) and to the Samaritans (Acts 8), and soon it would be opened to the Gentiles (Acts 10). Saul has moved off the scene, and Peter now returns. Soon Peter will move off the scene (except for a brief mention in Acts 15), and Paul will fill the pages of the book of Acts.

God changes His workmen, but His work goes on.

And you and I are privileged to be a part of that work today!

QUESTIONS FOR PERSONAL REFLECTION
OR GROUP DISCUSSION

1. What are some of the strengths of your church or group?

2. Read Acts 9:1–31. How did Jesus approach Saul? Why do you think He dealt with Saul like this?

3. Why did God use Ananias instead of one of the apostles to welcome Saul into the church?

4. What do you learn from God's use of Ananias? How is this relevant to you personally?

5. Why was Saul so bold for God?

6. How did people respond to Saul's conversion? Why?

7. What names are used for Christians in this chapter, and what is significant about each one?

8. How does each of these names affect our attitudes as Christians?

9. How did Luke describe the church at this point in history? How does your church compare with this description?

10. What can you do to help your church be more like what it is meant to be?

PETER'S MIRACLE MINISTRY

(Acts 9:32—10:48)

What is the greatest miracle that God can do for us? Some would call the healing of the body God's greatest miracle, while others would vote for the raising of the dead. However, I think that the greatest miracle of all is the salvation of a lost sinner. Why? Because salvation costs the greatest price, it produces the greatest results, and it brings the greatest glory to God.

In this section, we find Peter participating in all three miracles: He heals Aeneas, he raises Dorcas from the dead, and he brings the message of salvation to Cornelius and his household.

1. A GREAT MIRACLE—HEALING THE BODY (9:32–35)

The apostle Peter had been engaged in an itinerant ministry (Acts 8:25) when he found himself visiting the saints in Lydda, a largely Gentile city about twenty-five miles from Jerusalem. It is possible that the area had first been evangelized by people converted at Pentecost, or perhaps by faithful believers who had been scattered far and wide during the great persecution. No doubt Philip the evangelist had also ministered there (v. 40).

We know very little about Aeneas. How old was he? Did he believe on

Jesus Christ? Was he a Jew or a Gentile? All that Dr. Luke tells us is the man had been palsied for eight years, which meant he was crippled and helpless. He was a burden to himself and a burden to others, and there was no prospect that he would ever get well.

Peter's first miracle had been the healing of a crippled man (Acts 3), and now that miracle was repeated. As you read the book of Acts, you will see parallels between the ministries of Peter and Paul. Both healed cripples. Both were arrested and put into jail and were miraculously delivered. Both were treated like gods (Acts 10:25–26; 14:8–18), and both gave a bold witness before the authorities. Both had to confront false prophets (8:9–24; 13:6–12). No one reading the book of Acts could end up saying, "I am for Paul!" or "I am for Peter!" (1 Cor. 1:12). "But it is the same God which worketh all in all" (1 Cor. 12:6).

The resurrected Christ, by the authority of His name, brought perfect soundness to Aeneas (see Acts 3:6, 16; 4:10). The healing was instantaneous, and the man was able to get up and make his bed. He became a walking miracle! Acts 9:35 does not suggest that the entire population of Lydda and Sharon were saved, but only all those who had contact with Aeneas. Just seeing him walk around convinced them that Jesus was alive and they needed to trust in Him. (See John 12:10–11 for a similar instance.)

You can be sure that Peter did much more in Lydda than heal Aeneas, as great and helpful as that miracle was. He evangelized, taught, and encouraged the believers, and sought to establish the church in the faith. Jesus had commissioned Peter to care for the sheep (John 21:15–17), and Peter was faithful to fulfill that commission.

2. A GREATER MIRACLE—RAISING THE DEAD (9:36–43)

Joppa, the modern Jaffa, is located on the seacoast, some ten miles beyond Lydda. The city is important in Bible history as the place from which the prophet Jonah embarked when he tried to flee from God (Jonah 1:1–3).

Jonah went to Joppa to avoid going to the Gentiles, but Peter in Joppa received his call to go to the Gentiles! Because Jonah disobeyed God, the Lord sent a storm that caused the Gentile sailors to fear. Because Peter obeyed the Lord, God sent the "wind of the Spirit" to the Gentiles and they experienced great joy and peace. What a contrast!

It seemed so tragic that a useful and beloved saint like Dorcas (Tabitha = gazelle) should die when she was so greatly needed by the church. This often happens in local churches, and it is a hard blow to take. In my own pastoral ministry, I have experienced the loss of choice saints who were difficult to replace in the church, yet all we can say is, "The LORD gave, and the LORD hath taken away; blessed be the name of the LORD" (Job 1:21).

The believers in Joppa heard that Peter was in the area, and they sent for him immediately. There is no record in Acts that any of the apostles had raised the dead, so their sending for Peter was an evidence of their faith in the power of the risen Christ. When our Lord ministered on earth, He raised the dead, so why would He not be able to raise the dead from His exalted throne in glory?

We usually think of the apostles as leaders who told other people what to do, but often the people commanded them! (For Peter's "philosophy of ministry" read 1 Peter 5.) Peter was a leader who served the people and was ready to respond to their call. Peter had the power to heal, and he used the power to glorify God and help people, not to promote himself.

It was a Jewish custom first to wash the dead body, and then to anoint it with spices for burial. When Peter arrived in the upper room where Dorcas lay in state, he found a group of weeping widows who had been helped by her ministry. Keep in mind that there was no "government aid" in those days for either widows or orphans, and needy people had to depend on their "network" for assistance. The church has an obligation to help people who are truly in need (1 Tim. 5:3–16; James 1:27).

The account of Peter's raising of Dorcas should be compared with the account of our Lord's raising of Jairus's daughter (Mark 5:34–43). In both cases, the mourning people were put out of the room, and the words spoken are almost identical: *"talitha cumi:* little girl, arise"; *"Tabitha cumi:* Tabitha, arise." Jesus took the girl by the hand before He spoke to her, for He was not afraid of becoming ceremonially defiled, and Peter took Dorcas by the hand after she had come to life. In both instances, it was the power of God that raised the person from the dead, for the dead person certainly could not exercise faith.

As with the healing of Aeneas, the raising of Dorcas attracted great attention and resulted in many people trusting Jesus Christ. During the "many days" that he tarried in Joppa, Peter took the opportunity to ground these new believers in the truth of the Word, for faith built on miracles alone is not substantial.

It was a good thing Peter tarried in Joppa, because God met with him there in a thrilling new way. God's servants need not always be "on the go." They should take time to be alone with God, to reflect and meditate and pray, especially after experiencing great blessings. Yes, there were plenty of sick people Peter might have visited and healed, but God had other plans. He deliberately detained His servant in Joppa to prepare him for his third use of "the keys."

It is significant that Peter stayed in the home of a tanner, because tanners were considered "unclean" by the Jewish rabbis (see Lev. 11:35–40). God was moving Peter a step at a time from Jewish legalism into the freedom of His wonderful grace.

3. The Greatest Miracle—Winning Lost Sinners (10:1–48)

Chapter 10 is pivotal in the book of Acts, for it records the salvation of the Gentiles. We see Peter using "the keys of the kingdom" for the third and last time. He had opened the door of faith for the Jews (Acts 2) and also for the Samaritans (Acts 8), and now he would be used of God to bring the Gentiles into the church (see Gal. 3:27–28; Eph. 2:11–22).

This event took place about ten years after Pentecost. Why did the apostles wait so long before going to the lost Gentiles? After all, in His Great Commission (Matt. 28:19–20), Jesus had told them to go into *all* the world, and it would seem logical for them to go to their Gentile neighbors as soon as possible. But God has His times as well as His plans, and the transition from the Jews to the Samaritans to the Gentiles was a gradual one.

The stoning of Stephen and the subsequent persecution of the church marked the climax of the apostles' witness to the Jews. Then the gospel moved to the Samaritans. When God saved Saul of Tarsus, He got hold of His special envoy to the Gentiles. Now was the time to open the door of faith (Acts 14:27) to the Gentiles and bring them into the family of God.

There were four acts to this wonderful drama.

(1) Preparation (vv. 1–22). Before He could save the Gentiles, God had to prepare Peter to bring the message and Cornelius to hear the message. Salvation is a divine work of grace, but God works through human channels. Angels can deliver God's messages to lost men, but they cannot preach the gospel to them. That is our privilege—and responsibility.

Caesarea is sixty-five miles northwest of Jerusalem and thirty miles north of Joppa (Jaffa). At that time, Caesarea was the Roman capital of Judea and boasted of many beautiful public buildings. In that city lived Cornelius, the Roman centurion, whose heart had tired of pagan myths and empty religious rituals, and who had turned to Judaism in hopes he could find salvation. Cornelius was as close to Judaism as he could get without becoming a proselyte. There were many "God fearers" like him in the ancient world (Acts 13:16), and they proved to be a ready field for spiritual harvest.

It is interesting to see how religious a person can be and still not be saved.

Certainly, Cornelius was sincere in his obedience to God's law, his fasting, and his generosity to the Jewish people (compare this to Luke 7:1–10). He was not permitted to offer sacrifices in the temple, so he presented his prayers to God as his sacrifices (Ps. 141:1–2). In every way, he was a model of religious respectability—and yet he was not a saved man.

The difference between Cornelius and many religious people today is this: He knew that his religious devotion was not sufficient to save him. Many religious people today are satisfied that their character and good works will get them to heaven, and they have no concept either of their own sin or of God's grace. In his prayers, Cornelius was asking God to show him the way of salvation (Acts 11:13–14).

In many respects, John Wesley was like Cornelius. He was a religious man, a church member, a minister, and the son of a minister. He belonged to a "religious club" at Oxford, the purpose of which was the perfecting of the Christian life. Wesley served as a foreign missionary, but even as he preached to others, he had no assurance of his own personal salvation.

On May 24, 1738, Wesley reluctantly attended a small meeting in London where someone was reading aloud from Martin Luther's commentary on Romans. "About a quarter before nine," Wesley wrote in his journal, "while he was describing the change which God works in the heart through faith in Christ, I felt my heart strangely warmed, I felt I did trust in Christ, Christ alone for salvation; and an assurance was given me that He had taken away my sins, even mine, and saved me from the law of sin and death." The result was the great Wesleyan revival that not only swept many into the kingdom, but also helped transform British society through Christian social action.

God sent an angel to instruct Cornelius, and in true military fashion, Cornelius immediately obeyed. But why send for Peter, who was thirty miles away in Joppa, when Philip the evangelist was already in Caesarea (Acts 8:40)? Because it was Peter, not Philip, who had been given the "keys." God not only works at the right time, but He also works through the right servant, and both are essential.

Peter also had to be prepared for this event, since he had lived as an orthodox Jew all of his life (Acts 10:14). The law of Moses was a wall between the Jews and the Gentiles, and this wall had been broken down at the cross (Eph. 2:14–18). The Gentiles were considered aliens and strangers as far as the Jewish covenants and promises were concerned (vv. 11–13). But now, all of that would change, and God would declare that, as far as the Jew and the Gentile were concerned, "There is no difference" either in condemnation (Rom. 3:22–23) or in salvation (10:12–13).

Why did God use a vision about food to teach Peter that the Gentiles were not unclean? For one thing, Peter was hungry, and a vision about food would certainly "speak to his condition," as the Quakers say. Second, the distinction between "clean and unclean foods" was a major problem between the Jews and the Gentiles in that day. In fact, Peter's Christian friends criticized him for eating with the Gentiles (Acts 11:1–3)! God used this centuries-old regulation (Lev. 11) to teach Peter an important spiritual lesson.

A third reason goes back to something Jesus had taught Peter and the other disciples when He was ministering on earth (Mark 7:1–23). At that time, Peter did not fully understand what Jesus was saying, but now it would all come together. God was not simply changing Peter's diet; He was changing His entire program! The Jew was not "clean" and the Gentile "unclean," but *both Jew and Gentile were "unclean" before God!* "For God hath concluded them all in unbelief, that he might have mercy on all" (Rom. 11:32). This meant that a Gentile did not have to become a Jew in order to become a Christian.

Even though Peter's refusal was in the most polite terms, it was still wrong. Dr. W. Graham Scroggie wrote, "You can say 'No,' and you can say 'Lord'; but you cannot say 'No, Lord!'" If He is truly our Lord, then we can only say "Yes!" to Him and obey His commands.

God's timing is always perfect, and the three men from Caesarea arrived at the door just as Peter was pondering the meaning of the vision. The Spirit commanded Peter to meet the men and go with them. The phrase "doubting nothing" (Acts 10:20) means "making no distinctions." You find it again in Acts 11:12, and a similar word is used in Acts 11:2 ("contended with him" = "made a difference"). Peter was no longer to make any distinctions between the Jews and the Gentiles.

(2) Explanation (vv. 23–33). The fact that Peter allowed the Gentiles to lodge with him is another indication that the walls were coming down. Peter selected six Jewish believers to go along as witnesses (Acts 11:12), three times the official number needed. It would take at least two days to cover the thirty miles between Joppa and Caesarea. When Peter arrived, he discovered that Cornelius had gathered relatives and friends to hear the message of life. He was a witness even before he became a Christian!

How easy it would have been for Peter to accept honor and use the situation to promote himself, but Peter was a servant, not a celebrity (1 Peter 5:1–6). When he announced that he did not consider the Gentiles unclean, this must have amazed and rejoiced the hearts of his listeners. For centuries the Jews, on the basis of Old Testament law, had declared the Gentiles to be unclean, and some Jews even referred to the Gentiles as "dogs."

The remarkable thing in this section is Peter's question, "I ask, therefore, for what intent ye have sent for me?" (Acts 10:29). Didn't Peter know that he had been summoned there to preach the gospel? Had he forgotten the Acts 1:8 commission to go to "the uttermost part of the earth"? Today, we can look back at developing events in the church and understand what God was doing, but it might not have been that easy had we been living in the midst of those events. In fact, the Jerusalem church questioned Peter about his actions (11:1–18), and later called a conference to deal with the place of the Gentiles in the church (Acts 15).

Cornelius rehearsed his experience with the angel and then told Peter why he had been summoned: to tell him, his family, and his friends how they could be saved (Acts 11:14). They were not interested Gentiles asking for a lecture on Jewish religion. They were lost sinners begging to be told how to be saved.

Before we leave this section, some important truths must be emphasized. First, the idea that "one religion is as good as another" is completely false. Those who tell us that we should worship "the God of many names" and not "change other people's religions" are going contrary to Scripture. "Salvation is of the Jews" (John 4:22), and there can be no salvation apart from faith in Jesus Christ, who was born a Jew. Cornelius had piety and morality, but he did not have salvation. Some might say, "Leave Cornelius alone! His religion is a part of his culture, and it's a shame to change his culture!" God does not see it that way. Apart from hearing the message of the gospel and trusting Christ, Cornelius had no hope.

Second, the seeking Savior (Luke 19:10) will find the seeking sinner (Jer. 29:13). Wherever there is a searching heart, God responds. This is why it is essential that we as God's children obey His will and share His Word. You never know when your witness for Christ is exactly what somebody has been waiting and praying for.

Third, Peter certainly was privileged to minister to a model congregation (Acts 10:33). They were all present, they wanted to hear the Word, and they listened, believed, and obeyed. What more could a preacher ask?

(3) Proclamation (vv. 34–43). There can be no faith apart from the Word (Rom. 10:17), and Peter preached that Word. God is no respecter of persons as far as nationality and race are concerned. When it comes to sin and salvation, "there is no difference" (2:11; 3:22–23; 10:1–13). All men have the same Creator (Acts 17:26), and all men need the same Savior (4:12). Acts 10:35 does not teach that we are saved by works, otherwise Peter would be contradicting himself (Acts v. 43). To "fear God and work righteousness" is a description of the Christian life. To fear God is to reverence and trust Him (Mic. 6:8). The evidence of this faith is a righteous walk.

Peter then summarized the story of the life, death, and resurrection of Jesus Christ. Cornelius and his friends knew about Christ's life and death, for "this thing was not done in a corner" (Acts 26:26). Peter made it clear that Israel was God's instrument for accomplishing His work (10:36), but that Jesus is "Lord of all," and not just Lord of Israel. From the very founding of the nation of Israel, God made it clear that the blessing would be from Israel to the whole world (Gen. 12:1–3).

The public at large knew about Christ's life, ministry, and death, but only the apostles and other believers were witnesses of His resurrection. As in his previous sermons, Peter laid the blame for the crucifixion on the Jewish leaders (Acts 3:15; 4:10; 5:30), as did Stephen (7:52). Paul would pick up this same emphasis (1 Thess. 2:14–16).

Having finished this recitation of the historical basis for the gospel message, Christ's death and resurrection, Peter then announced the good news: "Whosoever believeth in him shall receive remission of sins" (Acts 10:43; see 2:21). His hearers laid hold of that word *whosoever*, applied it to themselves, believed on Jesus Christ, and were saved.

(4) Vindication (vv. 44–48). Peter was just getting started in his message when his congregation believed and the Holy Spirit interrupted the meeting (Acts 11:15). God the Father interrupted Peter on the Mount of Transfiguration (Matt. 17:4–5), and God the Son interrupted him in the matter of the temple tax (Matt. 17:24–27). Now, God the Spirit interrupted him—and Peter never was able to finish his sermon! Would that preachers today had interruptions of this kind!

The Holy Spirit was giving witness to the six Jews who were present that these Gentiles were truly born again. After all, these men had not seen the vision with Peter, and they needed to understand that the Gentiles were now on an equal footing with the Jews. This does not suggest that every new believer gives evidence of salvation by speaking in tongues, though every true believer will certainly use his or her tongue to glorify God (Rom. 10:9–10). This was an event parallel to Pentecost: The same Spirit who had come on the Jewish believers had now come on the Gentiles (Acts 11:15–17; 15:7–9). No wonder the men were astonished!

With this event, the period of transition in the early history of the church comes to an end. Believers among the Jews, Samaritans, and Gentiles have all received the Spirit of God and are united in the body of Christ (1 Cor. 12:13; Gal. 3:27).

These Gentiles were not saved by being baptized; they were baptized because they gave evidence of being saved. To use Acts 2:38 to teach salvation by baptism, or Acts 8:14–16 to teach salvation by the laying on of hands, is to ignore the transitional character of God's program. Sinners have always been saved by faith; that is one principle God has never changed. But God does change His methods of operation, and this is clearly seen in Acts 1—10. The experience of Cornelius and his household makes it very clear that baptism is not essential for salvation. From now on, the order will be hear the Word, believe on Christ, and receive the Spirit, and then be baptized and unite with other believers in the church to serve and worship God.

Peter tarried in Caesarea and helped to ground these new believers in the truth of the Word. Perhaps Philip assisted him. This entire experience is an illustration of the commission of Matthew 28:19–20. Peter went where God sent him and made disciples ("teach") of the Gentiles. Then he baptized them and taught them the Word.

That same commission applies to the church today. Are we fulfilling it as we should?

QUESTIONS FOR PERSONAL REFLECTION OR GROUP DISCUSSION

1. Has God ever done something miraculous for you? If so, what? Why is this action significant for you?

2. Read Acts 9:32—10:48 to find the three miracles God did for the early church. How did God use these miracles to further the gospel?

3. What kind of man was Cornelius?

4. How did God prepare Peter to take the gospel to Cornelius? Why was this necessary?

5. According to Wiersbe, what are the steps necessary for participating in the miracle of bringing people to Christ? Why is each step necessary?

6. Which of these steps, if any, have been barriers for you as you have sought to bring people to Christ? Please explain.

7. What can you use from Peter's message to Cornelius to share the gospel with people you know?

8. What are some other examples from the book of Acts in which God brought seeking sinners into contact with the gospel?

9. How will you make yourself available to God this week to talk to others about Him and His salvation?

Chapter Eleven

MAKING ROOM FOR THE GENTILES

(Acts 11)

Acts 11 describes how the church in Jerusalem related to "the saints below," the Gentiles in Caesarea and Antioch who had trusted Jesus Christ as their Savior and Lord. Having fellowship with the Gentiles was a new experience for these Jewish Christians, who all their lives had looked on the Gentiles as pagans and outsiders. Tradition said that a Gentile had to "become a Jew" in order to be accepted, but now Jews and Gentiles were united in the church through faith in Jesus Christ (Gal. 3:26–28).

Acts 11 describes three responses of the Jewish believers to the Gentile Christians. As you study these responses, you will better understand how Christians today ought to relate to one another.

1. THEY ACCEPTED THE GENTILES (11:1–18)

Peter no sooner returned to Jerusalem when he was met by members of the strong legalistic party in the church of Judea ("they that were of the circumcision") who rebuked him for fellowshipping with Gentiles and eating with them. Keep in mind that these Jewish believers did not yet understand the relationship between law and grace, Jews and

Gentiles, and Israel and the church. Most Christians today understand these truths, but, after all, we have Romans, Galatians, Ephesians, and Hebrews! There were many converted priests in the church who would be zealous for the law (Acts 6:7), and even the ordinary Jewish believer would have a difficult time making the transition (21:20). It was not only a matter of religion, but also of culture, and cultural habits are very hard to break.

The phrase "contended with him" comes from the same word translated "doubting nothing" in Acts 10:20 and 11:12. It means "to make a difference." These legalists were making a difference between the Gentiles and the Jews after Peter had demonstrated that "there is no difference!" God had declared the Gentiles "clean," that is, accepted before God on the same basis as the Jews—through faith in Jesus Christ.

Peter had nothing to fear. After all, he had only followed orders from the Lord, and the Spirit had clearly confirmed the salvation of the Gentiles. Peter reviewed the entire experience from beginning to end, and when he was finished, the Jewish legalists dropped their charges and glorified God for the salvation of the Gentiles (Acts 11:18). However, this did not end the matter completely, for this same legalistic party later debated with Paul about the salvation of the Gentiles (14:26—15:2). Even after the Jerusalem Conference, legalistic teachers continued to attack Paul and invade the churches he founded. They wanted to woo the believers into a life of obedience to the law (Gal. 1:6ff.; Phil. 3:1–3, 17–21). It is possible that many of these legalists were genuine believers, but they did not understand their freedom in Jesus Christ (Gal. 5:1ff.).

In his personal defense in Acts 11, Peter presented three pieces of evidence: the vision from God (Acts 11:5–11), the witness of the Spirit (vv. 12–15, 17), and the witness of the Word (v. 16). Of course, none of these men had seen the vision, but they trusted Peter's report, for they knew that he had been as orthodox as they in his personal life (10:14). He was not likely to go to the Gentiles on his own and then invent a story to back it up.

The witness of the Spirit was crucial, for this was God's own testimony that He had indeed saved the Gentiles. It is interesting that Peter had to go *all the way back to Pentecost* to find an example of what happened in the home of Cornelius! This suggests that a dramatic "baptism of the Spirit" (Acts 11:16), accompanied by speaking in tongues, was not an everyday occurrence in the early church. Peter could not use the experience of the Samaritans as his example, because the Samaritans received the gift of the Spirit through the laying on of the apostles' hands (8:14–17). Cornelius and his household received the Spirit the moment they trusted Christ. This is the pattern for today.

"What was I, that I could withstand God?" asked Peter, and to this question, the legalists had no answer. From beginning to end, the conversion of the Gentiles was God's gracious work. He gave them the gift of repentance and the gift of salvation when they believed. In later years, God would use the letters of Paul to explain the "one body," how believing Jews and believing Gentiles are united in Christ (Eph. 2:11—3:12). But at that time, this "mystery" was still hidden, so we must not be too hard on those saints who were uneasy about the place of the Gentiles in the church.

Christians are to receive one another and not dispute over cultural differences or minor matters of personal conviction (Rom. 14—15). Some of the Jewish Christians in the early church wanted the Gentiles to become Jews, and some of the Gentile believers wanted the Jews to stop being Jews and become Gentiles! This attitude can create serious division in the church even today, so it is important that we follow the example of Acts 11:18 and the admonition of Romans 14:1, and receive those whom God has also received.

2. THEY ENCOURAGED THE GENTILES (11:19–26)

When the saints were scattered abroad during Saul's persecution of the church (Acts 8:1), some of them ended up in Antioch, the capital of Syria, three hundred miles north of Jerusalem. (Don't confuse this city with Antioch in Pisidia, Acts 13:14.) There were at least sixteen Antiochs in the ancient world, but this one was the greatest.

With a population of half a million, Antioch ranked as the third largest city in the Roman Empire, following Rome and Alexandria. Its magnificent buildings helped give it the name "Antioch the Golden, Queen of the East." The main street was more than four miles long, paved with marble, and lined on both sides by marble colonnades. It was the only city in the ancient world at that time that had its streets lighted at night.

A busy port and a center for luxury and culture, Antioch attracted all kinds of people, including wealthy retired Roman officials who spent their days chatting in the baths or gambling at the races. With its large cosmopolitan population and its great commercial and political power, Antioch presented to the church an exciting opportunity for evangelism.

Antioch was a wicked city, perhaps second only to Corinth. Though all the Greek, Roman, and Syrian deities were honored, the local shrine was dedicated to Daphne, whose worship included immoral practices. "Antioch was to the Roman world what New York City is to ours," writes James A. Kelso in *An Archaeologist Follows the Apostle Paul*. "Here where all the gods of antiquity were worshipped, Christ must be exalted." Not only was an effective church built in Antioch, but it became the church that sent Paul out to win the Gentile world for Christ.

When the persecuted believers arrived in Antioch, they did not at all feel intimidated by the magnificence of the buildings or the pride of the citizens. The Word of God was on their lips and the hand of God was on their witness, and "a great number" of sinners repented and believed. It was a thrilling work of God's wonderful grace.

The church leaders in Jerusalem had a responsibility to "shepherd" the scattered flock, which now included Gentile congregations as far away as Syria. Apparently the apostles were ministering away from Jerusalem at the time, so the elders commissioned Barnabas to go to Antioch to find out what was going on among the Gentiles. This proved to be a wise choice, for Barnabas lived up to his nickname, "son of encouragement" (Acts 4:36 NASB).

Acts 11:24 gives us a "spiritual profile" of Barnabas, and he appears to be the kind of Christian all of us would do well to emulate. He was a righteous man who obeyed the Word in daily life so that his character was above reproach. He was filled with the Spirit, which explains the effectiveness of his ministry. That he was a man of faith is evident from the way he encouraged the church and then encouraged Saul. New Christians and new churches need people like Barnabas to encourage them in their growth and ministry.

How did Barnabas encourage these new Gentile believers? For one thing, he rejoiced at what he saw. Worshipping with Gentiles was a new experience for him, but he approached it positively and did not look for things to criticize. It was a work of God, and Barnabas gave thanks for God's grace.

He emphasized dedication of the heart as he taught the people the Word of God. The phrase "cleave [cling] to the Lord" does not suggest that they were to "keep themselves saved." The same grace that saves us can also keep us (1 Cor. 15:10; Heb. 13:9). The phrase reminds us of Joshua's admonition to Israel in Joshua 22:5. To "cleave to the Lord" includes loving the Lord, walking in His ways, obeying His Word, and serving Him wholeheartedly. It means that we belong to Him alone and that we cultivate our devotion to Him. "No man can serve two masters" (Matt. 6:24).

There were two wonderful results from Barnabas's work in Antioch. First, the church's witness made a great impact on the city so that "many people were added to the Lord" (Acts 11:24 NKJV). When the saints are grounded in the Word, they will have a strong witness to the lost, and there will be a balance in the church between edification and evangelism, worship and witness, teaching and testifying.

Second, the growth of the church meant that Barnabas needed help, so he went to Tarsus and enlisted Saul. But why go so far away just to find an assistant? Why not send to Jerusalem and ask the deacon Nicolas, who was from Antioch (Acts 6:5)? Because Barnabas knew that God had commissioned Saul to minister to the Gentiles (9:15; 22:21; 26:17). You recall that Barnabas befriended Saul in Jerusalem (9:26–27), and no doubt the two of them often talked about Saul's special call from God.

Saul had been converted about ten years when Barnabas brought him to Antioch. The New Testament does not tell us what Saul did back home in Tarsus after he left Jerusalem (Acts 9:28–30), but it is likely he was busy evangelizing both Jews and Gentiles. It may have been during this period that he founded the churches in Cilicia (15:23, 41; Gal. 1:21), and that he experienced some of the sufferings listed in 2 Corinthians 11:23–28. As he witnessed in the synagogues, you can be sure he would not have had an easy time of it!

What Barnabas did for Saul needs to be practiced in our churches today. Mature believers need to enlist others and encourage them in their service for the Lord. It was one of D. L. Moody's policies that each new Christian be given a task soon after conversion. At first, it might be only passing out hymnals or ushering people to their seats, but each convert had to be busy. As previously mentioned, he said, "It is better to put ten men to work than to do the work of ten men." Many of Mr. Moody's "assistants" became effective Christian workers in their own right, and this multiplied the witness.

It was at Antioch that the name *Christian* was first applied to the disciples of Jesus Christ. The Latin suffix -*ian* means "belonging to the party of." In derision, some of the pagan citizens of Antioch joined this Latin suffix to the Hebrew name "Christ" and came up with *Christian*. The name is found only three times in the entire New Testament: Acts 11:26; 26:28; 1 Peter 4:16.

Unfortunately, the word *Christian* has lost a great deal of significance over the centuries and no longer means one who has turned from sin, trusted Jesus Christ, and received salvation by grace (Acts 11:21–26). Many people who have never been born again consider themselves "Christians" simply because they say they are not "pagans." After all, they may belong to a church, attend services somewhat regularly, and even occasionally give to the work of the church! But it takes more than that for a sinner to become a child of God. It takes repentance from sin and faith in Jesus Christ, who died for our sins on the cross and rose again to give us eternal life.

The believers in the early church *suffered* because they were Christians (1 Peter 4:16). Dr. David Otis Fuller has asked, "If you were arrested for being a Christian, would there be enough evidence to convict you?" A good question! And the answer is a matter of life or death!

3. They Received Help from the Gentiles (11:27–30)

The foundation for the church was laid by the apostles and prophets (Eph. 2:20), and then both eventually moved off the scene. After all, you don't keep laying the foundation! The New Testament prophets received their messages from the Lord by the Holy Spirit, and delivered them to the people, sometimes in a tongue. The message would then have to be interpreted, after which the people would evaluate the message to make sure it came from God (see 1 Cor. 12:10; 14:27–33; 1 Thess. 5:19–21).

The New Testament prophets received their messages from the Lord *immediately*, but ministers and teachers today get their messages *mediately* through the Scriptures. We today have the completed Word of God from which the Holy Spirit teaches and guides us. First Corinthians 12:10 ties together the gifts of prophecy, discernment, and tongues and the interpretation of tongues. Of course, the Spirit is sovereign and can give to a believer any gift He desires (1 Cor. 12:11), but the passing of apostles and prophets from the scene, and the completing of God's revelation in the Word, suggest that a change has taken place.

There are people today who claim to receive special "words of revelation" or "words of wisdom" from the Lord, but such revelations are suspect and even dangerous. "To the law and to the testimony: if they speak not according to this word, it is because there is no light in them" (Isa. 8:20). "Hearken not unto the words of the prophets that prophesy unto you," warned Jeremiah. "They make you vain [fill you with false hopes]: they speak a vision of their own heart, and not out of the mouth of the LORD" (Jer. 23:16).

The Spirit told Agabus (see Acts 21:10–11) that a great famine was soon to come, and it did come during the reign of Claudius Caesar (AD 41–54), when crops were poor for many years. Ancient writers mention at least four famines: two in Rome, one in Greece, and one in Judea. The famine in Judea was especially severe, and the Jewish historian Josephus records that many people died for lack of money to buy what little food was available.

Agabus delivered his message to the Antioch believers, and they determined to help their fellow Christians in Judea. The purpose of true prophecy is not to satisfy our curiosity about the future but to stir up our hearts to do the will of God. The believers could not stop the famine from coming, but they could send relief to those in need.

An important spiritual principle is illustrated in this passage: If people have been a spiritual blessing to us, we should minister to them out of our material possessions. "Let him who is taught the word share in all good things with him who teaches" (Gal. 6:6 NKJV). The Jewish believers in Jerusalem had brought the gospel to Antioch. Then they had sent Barnabas to encourage the new believers. It was only right that the Gentiles in Antioch reciprocate and send material help to their Jewish brothers and sisters in Judea. Some years later, Paul would gather a similar offering from the Gentile churches and take it to the saints in Jerusalem (Acts 24:17; and see Rom. 15:23–28).

It is important to note that a change had taken place in the Jerusalem church. At one time, nobody in the church had any need (Acts 4:34), nor was it necessary to ask others for help. Those early years were "days of heaven on earth" as God richly blessed His people and used them as witnesses to the unbelieving nation. They were "times of refreshing" from the Lord (3:19). But when the message moved from the Jews to the Samaritans and the Gentiles, the Jerusalem "sharing program" gradually faded away and things became more normal.

The pattern for Christian giving today is not Acts 2:44–45 and 4:31–35 but Acts 11:29, "every man according to his ability." It is this pattern that Paul taught in 2 Corinthians 8—9. The practice of "Christian communism" was found only in Jerusalem and was a temporary measure while the message was going "to the Jew first." Like God's care of the Jews in the wilderness, it was a living exhibition of the blessings God would bestow if the nation would repent and believe.

The fact that the church elected Barnabas and Saul to take the relief offering to Jerusalem is evidence that they had confidence in them. The men had been working together in the teaching of the Word, and now they joined hands in the practical ministry of relieving the wants of the Jerusalem believers. No doubt they also ministered the Word along the way as they made the long journey from Antioch to Jerusalem. In a short time, the Spirit would call these two friends to join forces and take the gospel to the Gentiles in other lands (Acts 13:1ff.), and they would travel many miles together.

Another significant result from this ministry was the addition of John Mark to their "team" (Acts 12:25). It is likely that Mark was converted through the ministry of Peter (1 Peter 5:13). His mother's house was a gathering place for the Jerusalem believers (Acts 12:12), and she and Barnabas were related (Col. 4:10). Even though John Mark failed in his first "term" as a missionary (Acts 13:13), and helped cause a rift between Barnabas and Paul (Acts 15:38–40), he later became an effective assistant to Paul (2 Tim. 4:11) and was used of God to write the gospel of Mark.

The word *elders* in Acts 11:30 has not been used before in Acts, except to refer to the Jewish leaders (Acts 4:5, 23; 6:12). In the church, the elders were mature believers who had the spiritual oversight of the ministry (1 Peter 5:1; 2 John 1). When you compare Acts 20:17 and 28, and Titus 1:5 and 7, you learn that "elder" and "bishop" [overseer] are equivalent titles. The elders/bishops were the "pastors" of the flocks, assisted by the deacons, and the qualifications for both are found in 1 Timothy 3.

Wherever Paul established churches, he saw to it that qualified elders were ordained to give leadership to the assemblies (Acts 14:23; Titus 1:5). In the Jerusalem church, the apostles and elders gave spiritual oversight (Acts 15:2, 4, 6, 22). The delegation from the Antioch church did not ignore the spiritual leaders in Jerusalem, but delivered the gift to them for distribution to the needy members. This is an important principle and should be heeded in this day when so many organizations want to get support from local churches.

Was it a humbling experience for the Jewish believers to receive help from the Gentiles? Perhaps, but it was also a beautiful demonstration of love and a wonderful testimony of unity. Sir Winston Churchill said, "We make a living by what we get, but we make a life by what we give." It was an enriching experience for the churches in Jerusalem and in Antioch, for there is blessing both in giving and receiving when God's grace is in control.

It is unfortunate when individual Christians and local churches forget those who have been a spiritual blessing to them. The church at Antioch is a splendid example of how we as believers ought to show gratitude in a practical way to those who have helped us in our Christian life. Phillips Brooks was asked what he would do to revive a dead church, and he replied, "I would take up a missionary offering!"

Sincerely thinking of others is still the best formula for a happy and useful Christian life, both for individuals and for churches.

QUESTIONS FOR PERSONAL REFLECTION
OR GROUP DISCUSSION

1. How do you react when someone criticizes you?

2. Read Acts 11. What criticism was raised against Peter? Why?

3. What did Peter's answer teach those who disagreed with him?

4. What are some signs of a legalistic Christian or church?

5. Why was Barnabas chosen to investigate the reports of Antioch?

6. How did he encourage the believers there?

7. In what ways did Barnabas's bringing Saul to Antioch serve all parties?

8. How can you encourage others?

9. Who will you encourage this week, and how will you do it?

Chapter Twelve

WAKE UP TO A MIRACLE!

(Acts 12)

Imagine waking up to a miracle and having an angel for your alarm clock!

That's what happened to Peter when he was in prison for the third time, awaiting trial and certain death. Years later, when he wrote his first epistle, Peter may have had this miraculous experience in mind when he quoted Psalm 34:15–16: "For the eyes of the Lord are over the righteous, and his ears are open unto their prayers: but the face of the Lord is against them that do evil" (1 Peter 3:12). That quotation certainly summarizes what God did for Peter, and it reveals to us three wonderful assurances to encourage us in the difficult days of life.

1. GOD SEES OUR TRIALS (12:1–4)

"The eyes of the Lord are over the righteous" (1 Peter 3:12).

God watched and noted what Herod Agrippa I was doing to His people. This evil man was the grandson of Herod the Great, who ordered the Bethlehem children to be murdered, and the nephew of Herod Antipas, who had John the Baptist beheaded. A scheming and murderous family, the Herods were despised by the Jews, who resented having Edomites ruling over them. Of course, Herod knew this, so he persecuted the church to convince the Jewish people of his loyalty to the traditions of the fathers. Now that the Gentiles were openly a part of the church, Herod's plan was even more agreeable to the nationalistic Jews who had no place for "pagans."

Herod had several believers arrested, among them James, the brother of John, whom he beheaded. Thus James became the first of the apostles to be martyred. When you ponder his death in the light of Matthew 20:20–28, it takes on special significance. James and John, with their mother, had asked for thrones, but Jesus made it clear that there can be no glory apart from suffering. "Are ye able to drink of the cup that I shall drink of, and to be baptized with the baptism that I am baptized with?" He asked (Matt. 20:22). Their bold reply was, "We are able."

Of course, they did not know what they were saying, but they eventually discovered the high cost of winning a throne of glory: James was arrested and killed, and John became an exile on the Isle of Patmos, a prisoner of Rome (Rev. 1:9). Indeed, they did drink of the cup and share in the baptism of suffering that their Lord had experienced!

If it pleased the Jews when James was killed, just think how delighted they would be if Peter were slain! God permitted Herod to arrest Peter and put him under heavy guard in prison. Sixteen soldiers, four for each watch, kept guard over the apostle, with two soldiers chained to the prisoner and two watching the doors. After all, the last time Peter was arrested, he mysteriously got out of jail, and Herod was not about to let that happen again.

Why was James allowed to die, while Peter was rescued? After all, both were dedicated servants of God, needed by the church. The only answer is *the sovereign will of God,* the very thing Peter and the church had prayed about after their second experience of persecution (Acts 4:24–30). Herod had "stretched forth" his hand to destroy the church, but God would stretch forth His hand to perform signs and wonders and glorify His Son (Acts 4:28–30). God allowed Herod to kill James, but He kept him from harming Peter. It was the throne in heaven that was in control, not the throne on earth.

Please note that the Jerusalem church did not replace James as they had replaced Judas (Acts 1:15–26). As long as the gospel was going "to the Jew first," it was necessary to have the full complement of twelve apostles to witness to the twelve tribes of Israel. The stoning of Stephen ended that special witness to Israel, so the number of official witnesses was no longer important.

It is good to know that, no matter how difficult the trials or how disappointing the news, God is still on the throne and has everything under control. We may not always understand His ways, but we know His sovereign will is best.

2. GOD HEARS OUR PRAYERS (12:5–17)

"And his ears are open unto their prayers" (1 Peter 3:12).

The phrase "but prayer" is the turning point in the story. Never underestimate the power of a praying church! "The angel fetched Peter out of prison," said the Puritan preacher Thomas Watson, "but it was prayer that fetched the angel." Follow the scenes in this exciting drama in Acts 12.

Peter sleeping (vv. 5–6). If you were chained to two Roman soldiers and facing the possibility of being executed the next day, would you sleep very soundly? Probably not, but Peter did. In fact, Peter was so sound asleep that the angel had to strike him on the side to wake him up!

The fact that Peter had been a prisoner twice before is not what gave him his calm heart. For that matter, this prison experience was different from the other two. This time, he was alone, and the deliverance did not come right away. The other two times, he was able to witness, but this time, no special witnessing opportunities appeared. Peter's previous arrests had taken place after great victories, but this one followed the death of James, his dear friend and colleague. It was a new situation altogether.

What gave Peter such confidence and peace? To begin with, many believers were praying for him (Acts 12:12), and kept it up day and night for a week, and this helped to bring him peace (Phil. 4:6–7). Prayer has a way of reminding us of the promises of God's Word, such as "I will both lay me down in peace, and sleep: for thou, LORD, only makest me to dwell in safety" (Ps. 4:8). Or "Fear thou not, for I am with thee; be not dismayed; for I am thy God: I will strengthen thee; yea, I will help thee; yea, I will uphold thee with the right hand of my righteousness" (Isa. 41:10).

But the main cause of Peter's peace was the knowledge that Herod could not kill him. Jesus had promised Peter that he would live to be an old man and end his life crucified on a Roman cross (John 21:18–19). Peter simply laid hold of that promise and committed the entire situation to the Lord, and God gave him peace and rest. He did not know how or when God would deliver him, but he did know that deliverance was coming.

Peter obeying (vv. 7–11). Once again we behold the ministry of angels (Acts 5:19; 8:26; 10:3, 7) and are reminded that the angels care for God's children (Ps. 34:7). The angel brought light and liberty into the prison cell, but the guards had no idea that anything was going on. However, if Peter was going to be delivered, he had to obey what the angel commanded. He probably thought it was a dream or a vision, but he arose and followed the angel out of the prison and into the street Only then did he come to himself and realize that he had been a part of another miracle.

The angel commanded Peter to bind his garments with his girdle, and then to put on his sandals. These were certainly ordinary tasks to do while a miracle is taking place! But God often joins the miraculous with the ordinary just to encourage us to keep in balance. Jesus multiplied the loaves and fishes, but then commanded His disciples to gather up the leftovers. He raised Jairus's daughter from the dead, then told her parents to give her something to eat. Even in miracles, God is always practical.

God alone can do the extraordinary, but His people must do the ordinary. Jesus raised Lazarus from the dead, but the men had to roll the stone from the tomb. The same angel that removed the chains from Peter's hands could have put the shoes on Peter's feet, but he told Peter to do it. God never wastes miracles.

Peter had to stoop before he could walk. It was a good lesson in humility and obedience. In fact, from that night on, every time Peter put on his shoes, it must have reminded him of the prison miracle and encouraged him to trust the Lord.

This deliverance took place at Passover season, the time of year when the Jews celebrated their exodus from Egypt. The word *delivered* in Acts 12:11 is the same word Stephen used when he spoke about the Jewish exodus (7:34). Peter experienced a new kind of "exodus" in answer to the prayers of God's people.

Peter knocking (vv. 12–16). As Peter followed the angel, God opened the way, and when Peter was free, the angel vanished. His work was done, and now it was up to Peter to trust the Lord and use his common sense in taking the next step. Since it was the prayers of God's people that had helped to set him free, Peter decided that the best place for him would be in that prayer meeting at Mary's house. Furthermore, he wanted to report the good news that God had answered their prayers. So Peter headed for the house of Mary, mother of John Mark.

When you remember that (a) many people were praying, (b) they were praying earnestly, (c) they prayed night and day for perhaps as long as a week, and (d) their prayers were centered specifically on Peter's deliverance, then the scene that is described here is almost comical. The answer to their prayers is standing at the door, but they don't have faith enough to open the door and let him in! God could get Peter out of a prison, but Peter can't get himself into a prayer meeting!

Of course, the knock at the door might have been that of Herod's soldiers, coming to arrest more believers. It took courage for the maid Rhoda ("rose") to go to the door, but imagine her surprise when she recognized Peter's voice! She was so overcome that she forgot to open the door! Poor Peter had to keep knocking and calling while the "believers" in the prayer meeting decided what to do! And the longer he stood at the gate, the more dangerous his situation became.

The exclamation, "It is his angel" (Acts 12:15) reveals their belief in "guardian angels" (Matt. 18:10; Heb. 1:14). Of course, the logical question is, "Why would an angel bother to knock?" All he had to do was simply walk right in! Sad to say, good theology plus unbelief often leads to fear and confusion.

We must face the fact that even in the most fervent prayer meetings there is sometimes a spirit of doubt and unbelief. We are like the father who cried to Jesus, "Lord, I believe; help thou mine unbelief" (Mark 9:24). These Jerusalem saints believed that God could answer their prayers, so they kept at it night and day. But, when the answer came right to their door, they refused to believe it. God graciously honors even the weakest faith, but how much more He would do if only we would trust Him.

Note the plural pronouns in Acts 12:16: "They ... opened the door, and ... they were astonished." I get the impression that, for safety's sake, they decided to open the door *together* and face *together* whatever might be on the other side. Rhoda would have done it by herself, but she was too overcome with joy. It is commendable that a lowly servant girl recognized

Peter's voice and rejoiced that he was free. Rhoda surely was a believer who knew Peter as a friend.

Peter declaring (v. 17). Apparently everybody began to speak at once, and Peter had to silence them. He quickly gave an account of the miracle of his deliverance and no doubt thanked them for their prayer help. He instructed them to get the word to James, the half brother of the Lord, who was the leader of the Jerusalem assembly (Matt. 13:55; Acts 15:13ff.; Gal. 1:19). James was also the author of the epistle of James.

Where Peter went when he left the meeting, nobody knows to this day! It certainly was a well-kept secret. Except for a brief appearance in Acts 15, Peter walks off the pages of the book of Acts to make room for Paul and the story of his ministry among the Gentiles. First Corinthians 9:5 tells us that Peter traveled in ministry with his wife, and 1 Corinthians 1:12 suggests that he visited Corinth. There is no evidence in Scripture that Peter ever visited Rome. In fact, if Peter had founded the church in Rome, it is unlikely that Paul would have gone there, for his policy was to work where other apostles had not labored (Rom. 15:18–22). Also, he certainly would have said something to or about Peter when he wrote his letter to the Romans.

Before we leave this section, it would be profitable to consider how Christians can best pray for those in prison, for even today there are many people in prison only because they are Christians. "Remember them that are in bonds, as bound with them" commands Hebrews 13:3. In other words, pray for them as you would want them to pray for you if your situations were reversed.

We ought to pray that God will give them grace to bear with suffering so that they might have a triumphant witness for the Lord. We should ask the Spirit to minister the Word to them and bring it to their remembrance. It is right to ask God to protect His own and to give them wisdom as they must day after day deal with a difficult enemy. We must ask God that, if it is His will, they be delivered from their bondage and suffering and reunited with their loved ones.

3. GOD DEALS WITH OUR ENEMIES (12:18–25)

"But the face of the Lord is against them that do evil" (1 Peter 3:12).

If the account had ended with Peter's departure, we would find ourselves wondering, "What happened to the prison guards and to Herod?" We do not know at what time the angel delivered Peter, but when the next quaternion arrived at the cell, imagine their consternation when they discovered that the guards were there but the prisoner was gone! If the new watch awakened the old watch, it was certainly a rude awakening for them! If the old watch was already awake and alert, they must have had a difficult time explaining the situation to the new watch. How could a chained prisoner escape when there were four guards present and the doors were locked?

If a guard permitted a prisoner to escape, Roman law required that he receive the same punishment that the prisoner would have received, even if it was death (see Acts 16:27; 27:42). This law did not strictly apply in Herod's jurisdiction, so the king was not forced to kill the guards, but being a Herod, he did it anyway. Instead of killing one man to please the Jews, he killed four and perhaps hoped it would please them more.

"The righteous is delivered out of trouble, and the wicked cometh in his stead" (Prov. 11:8). This truth is illustrated in the death of Herod. While God does not always bring retribution this quickly, we can be sure that the Judge of all the earth will do what is right (Gen. 18:25; Rev. 6:9–11).

The people of Tyre and Sidon, who depended on the Jews for food (see Ezra 3:7), had in some way displeased King Herod and were in danger of losing this assistance. In true political fashion, they bribed Blastus, who was in charge of the king's bed chamber, and thus a trusted official; he in turn convinced the king to meet the delegation. It was an opportunity for the proud king to display his authority and glory, and for the delegates to please him with their flattery.

The Jewish historian Josephus said that this scene took place during a festival honoring Claudius Caesar, and that the king wore a beautiful silver garment in honor of the occasion. We do not know what Herod said in his oration, but we do know why he said it: He wanted to impress the people. And he did! They played on his Herodian ego and told him he was a god, and he loved every minute of it.

But he did not give the glory to the Lord, so this whole scene was nothing but idolatry. "I am the LORD: that is my name: and my glory will I not give to another" (Isa. 42:8; see 48:11). Instead of Peter being killed by Herod, it was Herod who was killed by Peter's God! Perhaps the same angel who delivered Peter also smote the king. Herod contracted some affliction in his bowels and died five days later, according to Josephus. This was in AD 44.

This event is more than a slice of ancient history, because it typifies the world and its people today. The citizens of Tyre and Sidon were concerned about one thing only—getting sufficient food to feed their stomachs. To be sure, food is essential to life, but when we pay any price to get that food, we are doing wrong. By flattering the king and calling him a god, the delegation knew they could get what they wanted.

I cannot help but see in King Herod an illustration of the future "Man of Sin" who will one day rule the world and persecute God's people (2 Thess. 2; Rev. 13). This "Man of Sin" (or Antichrist) will make himself god and will command the worship of the whole world. But Jesus Christ will return and judge him and those who follow him (Rev. 19:11–21).

The world still lives for praise and pleasure. Man has made himself his own god (Rom. 1:25). The world still lives on the physical and ignores the spiritual (see 1 John 2:15–17). It lives by force and flattery instead of faith and truth, and one day it will be judged.

The church today, like Israel of old, suffers because of people like Herod who use their authority to oppose the truth. Beginning with Pharaoh in Egypt, God's people have often suffered under despotic rulers and governments, and God has always preserved His witness in the world. God has not always judged evil officials as He judged Herod, but He has always watched over His people and seen to it that they did not suffer and die in vain. Our freedom today was purchased by their bondage.

The early church had no "political clout" or friends in high places to "pull strings" for them. Instead, they went to the highest throne of all, the throne of grace. They were a praying people, for they knew that God could solve their problems. God's glorious throne was greater than the throne of Herod, and God's heavenly army could handle Herod's weak soldiers any day or night! The believers did not need to bribe anyone at court. They simply took their case to the highest court and left it with the Lord!

And what was the result? "But the word of God grew and multiplied" (Acts 12:24). This is another of Luke's summaries, or "progress reports," that started with Acts 6:7 (see 9:31; 16:5; 19:20; 28:31). Luke is accomplishing the purpose of his book and showing us how the church spread throughout the Roman world from its small beginnings in Jerusalem. What an encouragement to us today!

At the beginning of Acts 12, Herod seemed to be in control, and the church was losing the battle. But at the end of the chapter, Herod is dead and the church—very much alive—is growing rapidly!

The secret? A praying church!

Missionary Isobel Kuhn used to pray when in trouble, "If this obstacle is from thee, Lord, I accept it; but if it is from Satan, I refuse him and all his works in the name of Calvary!" And Dr. Alan Redpath has often said, "Let's keep our chins up and our knees down—we're on the victory side!"

God works when churches pray, and Satan still trembles "when he sees the weakest saint upon his knees."

QUESTIONS FOR PERSONAL REFLECTION OR GROUP DISCUSSION

1. Describe a modern situation in which Christians are being persecuted because of their faith.

2. Read Acts 12. Why did Herod persecute the church?

3. How does the relationship between James' death and Peter's escape from prison emphasize the relationship between God's sovereign will and prayer?

4. Do you believe your prayers matter? Please explain.

5. What role did Peter's obedience play in his rescue? Why was that the case?

6. Why are we often surprised by God's answers to our prayers, as the church was at Peter's release from jail?

7. How do you think the church's prayer life might have been different after Peter's release?

8. What happened as a result of God's dealing with Herod?

9. How can your group be more involved in praying for one another?

10. What have you learned from this study of Acts 1—12 that has benefited you the most?

The "BE" series . . .

For years pastors and lay leaders have embraced Warren W. Wiersbe's very accessible commentary of the Bible through the individual "BE" series. Through the work of David C. Cook Global Mission, the "BE" series is part of a library of books made available to indigenous Christian workers. These are men and women who are called by God to grow the kingdom through their work with the local church worldwide. Here are a few of their remarks as to how Dr. Wiersbe's writings have benefited their ministry.

"Most Christian books I see are priced too high for me . . .
I received a collection that included 12 Wiersbe
commentaries a few months ago and I have
read every one of them.
I use them for my personal devotions every day and they
are incredibly helpful for preparing sermons.
The contribution David C. Cook is making to the
church in India is amazing."
—Pastor E. M. Abraham, Hyderabad, India